Flower Gardening in Kansas City

Secrets and tips from
the area's best gardeners

Craig Nienaber

Acknowledgments

It's obvious that this book was possible only because so many gardeners opened their gates to us. Thanks to all of them, not only for their time but also for their patience in trying to explain in a few hours everything they had learned in a lifetime. I haven't ever met a more pleasant group of people. They alone are a good argument for taking up gardening.

Finding all of them got a huge assist from three people who work with county Master Gardener programs. Dennis Patton in Johnson County, Mark Topping in Wyandotte County and Gloria Jenkins in Jackson County all helped me fill in the list of gardens to make sure I had a broad variety.

Our biggest stroke of luck occurred when Tim Janicke agreed to shoot the photos. Tim, a former photo editor for *The Kansas City Star* and now editor of *Star Magazine*, can shoot just about anything but the photos in this book are spectacular. He's a busy man who fortunately found time to visit more than 20 gardens and highlight the best in each, which isn't as easy as it may look.

On the production end, Doug Worgul calmly coordinated the project, Jo Ann Groves endured my endless questions about imaging, and Tim Engle copy edited, a job no one appreciates enough. Thanks to you all. And a last, major thanks to Kelly Ludwig, our delightful designer whose pages were so much better than I'd ever imagined they would be. She fought through a blizzard of e-mails and files, and she never freaked once.

Craig Nienaber

Flower Gardening in Kansas City
Secrets and tips from the area's best gardeners

Written and edited by Craig Nienaber
Photography by Tim Janicke
Design and production by Kelly Ludwig

Published by KANSAS CITY STAR BOOKS
1729 Grand Boulevard
Kansas City, Missouri USA 64108

First edition

Library of Congress Control Number: 2003113117

ISBN: 0974601217

Printed in the United States of America
By Walsworth Publishing Co.

To order copies call StarInfo, (816) 234-4636

For more information about this and other fine books from Kansas City Star Books visit our Web site at www.thekansascitystore.com.

Table of Contents

"Flowers appear on the earth; the season of singing has come."

— Song of Solomon, 2:12

Growing up, I didn't care much about flowers even though my mother had a wonderful rose garden in the back yard. I used it as a third baseline. Now, many years later, I care about flowers a lot more but I still don't know nearly as much as you might expect from the author of a gardening book.

That's why all the advice in this book comes from expert gardeners, not me. The purpose of the book is to let two dozen Kansas Citians share what they've learned through hard experience about flower gardening in this area. Except for two professionals in the final chapter, all the gardeners are strictly amateurs working in their own yards on their own time.

They are excellent gardeners, although not necessarily the best gardeners in Kansas City. That would be a different book and one sure to kick up some controversy — Kansas City has too many wonderful gardens to rank them. Instead, the people in this book are veterans selected to demonstrate many types of gardening. They range from a couple who have turned a pasture into a three-acre showpiece to an elderly man who now gardens in a tiny space at his new retirement home. They all face different challenges and possess different skills. I hope that some of them will inspire and help you, even if you only put out a few flowers in pots each spring.

My heartfelt thanks to the gardeners in this book. They volunteered their time and they were the most gracious hosts one could imagine. Besides that, they gave me enough great ideas to keep me busy for the next 10 years.

Thanks, too, to my wife, who with great humor endured a long year while I worked on the book on weekends, and has asked me to please not write another one for a while. And thanks to my mother for planting some images of flowers in my boyhood brain, and for the whole third baseline thing.

Craig Nienaber

English Garden

"You find a secret around every corner."

John and Connie Anderson
Leavenworth, Kansas

The Andersons have lived in their century-old home since 1991, when they began working on their garden. Connie is a deputy sheriff for Leavenworth County, but it's clear John isn't a local. His musical accent comes from Northumberland, a county in England near the Scottish border. Now retired from the British military, John does a lot of the work in the garden. "It's a full-time job," he says. He's also an experienced ornithologist who delights in the birds that visit and nest in the garden, including five varieties of hummingbirds alone. Connie works on both the outside and the inside of the house, an 1883 period piece that has been on several historical tours. Put it all together and it's no wonder the Andersons find peace sitting on the porch at night enjoying the garden. "This is what we do," says Connie.

The front gate of the Andersons' home leads to the winding paths of an English garden. Above, a Scottish rose.

6

Design

With John's background, it's no surprise that the Andersons laid out an English garden. Besides arbors and a white picket fence that took two years to build, the garden has gravel paths that wind around raised beds. (A garden that has straight paths but claims to be English is not to be trusted, John says.) Neatly trimmed shrubs accent the grounds, and plants jam together in the beds. Two advantages of packing flowers close: The sun won't scorch the plants, and the dense foliage holds moisture in the ground. But it can be a harder garden to work, too, because eventually the beds go wild, with some plants overrunning others. When that happens, it's time to dig them up and start over. "It's a full-time job," John says. "It's nowhere near where I want it to be."

Right, Connie and John Anderson at the front gate. Left, Labella snapdragons.

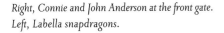

Favorites

The Andersons rely more on standard annuals than on exotic perennials. Among their workhorses:

Snapdragons. These provide a lot of stunning color. The Andersons use three varieties: rocket, which grows up to 4 feet; labella, a little shorter; and standard snaps, only about 8 inches. The rockets are stunning in early summer but may need to be staked. They're annuals that self-seed for next year. Cut them back to a few inches after they bloom, John says.

Petunias. They also provide color. Certainly they get leggy in the summer, John says, but after the first blooms, cut them back about 4 inches — to about a half-inch above where they branch. That will revive them and make them bushier. And don't forget to deadhead the spent blooms.

Hollyhocks. Hollyhocks give the garden great height, especially in raised beds. They self-seed prodigiously. To get them to grow up to 8 feet, John says, take off the bottom foot or more of their foliage, which sends the sap higher in the stalk. Those leaves only go yellow anyway, so no loss. Besides, you can just drop the leaves on the ground around the plant — they make good mulch.

Above, standard snapdragons. Right, petunias also give color to the garden.

Soil

Any aspiring gardener in this area needs to know that pervasive clay is a big problem, so don't think you're going to put a garden together in a year, Connie says. "If you're starting from scratch, plan on a long project with great rewards in a few years," she says. If the Andersons have a secret, it's the hard work they put into preparing the soil year after year.

Recipe for new gardens

Remove the clay and replace it with:

Half black dirt

Half sand

Mix that and add a quarter of spagnum peat.

That may seem like a lot of sand, but John swears by it as a clay-buster. Any sand will do, but he says silver sand works best because it has the sharpest edges.

Recipe for maintaining gardens

Each year the Andersons dig up their soil and add cow manure, peat and sometimes wood ash, which contains potassium and brings out the colors in flowers. They also may add some sand again and even shredded mulch to break up the clay. It's harder in perennial gardens, where you don't want to disturb the roots, but you can usually hoe down about 6 inches around the plant. Before winter, the Andersons spread white powdered lime on the garden. It sweetens soil and kills grubs, John says.

Above, John Anderson with the 'Flora McDonald' roses that grow along the fence. Left, a geranium, yellow marigolds and a red standard snapdragon.

*"No garden is finished —
you're always working on it."*

Honey Barnekoff
Overland Park, Kansas

In November 2003, Honey Barnekoff became the first woman
president of the national Gardeners of America/Men's Garden Clubs of
America. But she's only been gardening seriously in the dozen years since
moving into her current home. Before then she dedicated her time more to
music. Now she has shade gardens, sun gardens and a pond, thanks to help
from her husband, Tom, who notes, "We've created a monster." Honey also is
a Master Gardener who contributes her time to chairing a program that
teaches inmates at the penitentiary in Lansing how to garden. Honey retired
after many years at TWA, but she still spends time as a school crossing guard.
"Nature abhors a vacuum," says Honey, and so, it seems, does she.

*Even at dusk, an 1,800-square-foot garden lights up Honey Barnekoff's back yard. Hybrid lilies provide
whites and yellows while mulched pathways lead farther into the garden. Above, a tree peony.*

Philosophy

Honey designs her garden so that it changes every five weeks — something is always blooming. She mixes in plenty of annuals — 26 flats or more — that she starts from seed in her basement.

With so many plants, she tries to keep gardening simple. For example, when she dug an 1,800-square-foot garden in the middle of her back yard, she included mulched walking paths so she could tend the beds without stepping in them. Honey also uses lots of mulch and ground covers to cut down on weeding. She even lets vinca grow over many of her daylilies, letting it hold moisture in the ground. And she gave away her 47 hybrid tea roses — they required too much time.

Honey also tries to avoid chemical pesticides and herbicides. "Using chemicals is poor stewardship," she says. She suggests other options, such as using the pointy balls that fall from sweetgum trees to control slugs, which won't crawl over them.

Left, one of the stepping stones that Honey made and placed along a path in her huge center garden. Above, granddaughter Brittany Joanne (B.J.) joins Honey Barnekoff at a new back yard playhouse in part of the shade garden. Far left, a sign near the street welcomes visitors to Honey's impressive gardens — and she means it.

Favorites

Honey's garden is so large that it seems there's at least one of everything. But here are a few of her specialties:

Lilies. They catch a lot of attention Honey uses many varieties, including oriental, asiatic and hybrids. That way she can stretch bloom times from early to late in the season. Lilies aren't difficult, except that rabbits like to munch off the tops, so she has to protect many of them with chicken wire.

Columbine. Honey has many hybrid varieties, all stunning. They self-seed bountifully and bloom early. But keep the hybrids away from common columbine or the varieties will cross and all will turn common the next year.

Mountain laurel. A relative of azaleas that was common in the much milder climate of Kentucky, where she grew up. It shouldn't grow here, but she's had some of hers for eight years by creating "micro-climates" for them, giving them shade and protection using other plants. Don't be afraid, she says, to at least try plants that you shouldn't.

Left, columbines are one of Honey Barnekoff's favorite flowers, including this Rocky Mountain columbine (aquilegia caerulea). Above, a dwarf mountain laurel (kalmia latifolia `Elf'), another favorite.

Tips

Cheap annuals. If you want to start annuals indoors in the winter, try using two ordinary shop lights, one warm, the other cool. They are much cheaper than grow lights. Leave them on at least 16 hours a day. Keep a small fan oscillating to keep disease off the seedlings and give them a little stress. Once they're ready, leave them outside several days to harden them before planting.

Invasive plants. If you've got an invasive plant like lythrum, give it less of what it wants. Lythrum, for example, wants water, so just give it less and it spreads less. In the same way, ribbon grass can be controlled by putting it in a shady spot.

Droopy mums. To keep chrysanthemums from getting so tall they flop, cut them back not once but twice, each time about halfway down the stem. Also, you can stick the cuttings in a pot and they will root.

Don't crowd. Leave plenty of space between plants. Eventually they'll grow together on their own, and until then you won't need to spend as much time digging them up and transplanting them.

Right, a clematis ('henryii').
Far right, a tall bearded iris,
(iris germanica 'Beverly Sills').

More Tips

Pantyhose for plants. Strips of pantyhose are great for tying up vines. They're soft, so they don't damage stems, and they last forever. Depending on their color, they're also unobtrusive.

Fall planting. If you make your perennial flower beds in the fall, they'll be better than if you planted in spring. The new perennials will go dormant over the winter, settle in and be established by spring.

Use shade. Don't be afraid of putting sun plants in a spot with some shade. Kansas City is so hot that you can get away with it.

Resources

Honey recommends *Gardening in the Heartland* by the late Rachel Snyder as an excellent resource for Midwestern gardeners. Snyder, who lived in Prairie Village, was editor of *Flower and Garden* magazine for many years. The book provides a lot of useful information, such as whether plants are invasive or conflict with other plants.

Left, Honey Barnekoff shows a hybrid rugosa rose (rosa rugosa `Rotesmeer'). Above, foxglove (digitalis purpurea). Far left, common lavender iris backed by peonies.

An Outdoor Room

"I like things that are different."

Sandy Bonar
Prairie Village, Kansas

When Sandy and Don Bonar moved into their first home almost 20 years ago, it had a patio shaped like a piano, surrounded by a dozen yuccas. Don wanted roses instead, so they put in 18. "I went crazy," Sandy says, and it's been that way ever since. She had a head start when moving to their second home because she brought along 85 perennials. The back yard now abounds with flowers and what-the-heck sculptures framing an outdoor room the couple built to enjoy it all. Sandy has a little more time than she once did, retiring after 20 years at Hallmark, but she still works part time as an accountant. She's also a Master Gardener who teaches gardening workshops and belongs to one other organization, the Garden Center Association — down from the 10 groups she did belong to.

Purple coneflowers are among the flowers surrounding the Bonars' outdoor room.
Above, leaf lettuce in a pot.

Flowers for Walls

The Bonars' current Prairie Village home had a huge concrete patio in the back when they arrived. "You could have landed a helicopter there," Sandy says. They had to decide what to do with all that hard space and chose against a traditional gazebo, which seemed too ornate. Instead they built an outdoor room — Don did much of the work — with entirely open walls and enough space to comfortably fit furniture. A pergola brings electricity in from the house so they can enjoy music and entertain there.

Left, Sandy and Don Bonar enjoy the outdoor room they built. Above, rattlesnake master is one of the unusual plants Sandy Bonar enjoys.

Easing Back Pain

A few years ago Sandy developed some back problems, which made her adjust her gardening. Here are some of her discoveries to make gardening easier for herself and others with bad backs:

Prop the plants. Sandy puts tomato cages around her bigger perennials in the spring to keep them from flopping later. That way she doesn't have to stake and tie them. Sandy cuts the cages down to fit each plant so they're nearly invisible.

Raise the dirt. Don elevated the herb bed on the patio so Sandy doesn't have to bend too far. It helps to have a woodworker in the family.

Use more pots. You can raise them to any height, and they're just as attractive as the rest of the garden.

Replace flowers. Sandy took out one perennial bed on the side of the yard and put in shrubs and tall grasses, which require much less work.

A giant fish sculpture manages to hide in the back shrubbery.

Favorites

Lythrum. Sandy's favorite perennial. It's considered to be invasive, but it doesn't get enough water to be a problem in this area. It adds great color to the garden.

Joe Pye Weed. Sandy resisted it for years just because of the name. But now she has two. "It makes a statement in the garden," she says. The large perennial has unusual, fluffy flowers that bloom in the fall, when many other flowers have stopped. They need a lot of sun but they're a magnet for butterflies and bees.

Patrinia Nagoya. It's a perennial that she read about. It has tiny yellow blooms in the fall and interesting, serrated edges.

Shrub roses. Sandy has the Knock Out variety, as well as others. Knock Out is huge, hardy and has new blooms all summer.

Sweet Rocket. It's a biennial that blooms with a lot of lavender color in the early summer. It flowers the year after you plant it.

Below, calamagrostis `Karl Forrester' is a feather reed grass that blooms in June. Left, `Knockout,' a shrub rose.

Tips

Award winners. Pay attention to the annuals, perennials and bulbs of the year. Garden stores can point you to them, and so can other sources. Award winners are proven to be tough, and that's what you need in Kansas City. "We have heat, cold, drought and flood," Sandy says. "You need good performers under a variety of conditions."

You can't overdo soil preparation. "That was the hardest thing for me to learn," she says. "I added stuff but it was never enough." Now she doesn't skimp on the compost, which is from her own back yard. "The performance of perennials is in direct proportion to soil preparation," she says.

Colors. Be brave. Some gardeners don't like yellow, orange or red, but Sandy does. "Mother Nature makes no mistakes," she says. "I love the hot colors in my garden."

Containers. The biggest mistake people make with pots is to choose blah plants. Use foliage with a variety of shapes and colors, such as coleus. When putting containers together, Sandy often picks up coleus plants at garden stores and walks around with them to find plants that pick up those colors.

Wood mulch has drawbacks. Sandy tried using it last year to reduce weeding but won't again. It kept seeds from self-sowers like larkspur from germinating.

Rudbeckia. It's tempting to let it go, but divide it every year. Otherwise it gets too big.

Azaleas. Sandy has eight of them, but they're not easy. Roots are shallow and need lots of water. "I would never recommend it here in Kansas City without a sprinkler system," she says.

Right, the outdoor room seen through an arbor covered by pipe vine. Above, Sandy Bonar at the gate her husband made to the back yard.

"I want my garden to be a calming presence."

Norma Boyer
Kansas City, Missouri

Norma Boyer admits to more than her share of gardening failures. Creating a calming presence isn't one of them. Sometimes she sits with clients — she works with people in career transition — in an outdoor room between her two decks where they can enjoy the tranquility of a back yard filled with flowers. The view bleeds over into surrounding yards, where neighbors maintain wonderful gardens, too. Her own small yard extends in other ways as well because Norma, a Master Gardener, finds one of her greatest joys in sharing her plants with neighbors and other friends. "My garden is for peace, meditation and sharing," she says.

Norma Boyer with her cat, Flash Gordon, on one of her decks. Above, a wild geranium.

Challenges

Norma has limited time and space, so her approach to gardening is simple:

"You do it when you have time and hope it works." But in the years since 1988, when she and her husband, Arthur Lowell, moved into their house, the lot has undergone a transformation. To deal with the space issue, especially in the back yard, Norma simply replaced the lawn with flower beds. "I'm not interested in having grass," she says. She also added vertical space by using her high deck, adding a low deck, and turning an open carport in between into an outdoor room with a tropical mural painted by a friend, local artist Amy Harvey.

As for time, Norma cuts a few corners. For example, she fertilizes in the spring or when she thinks about it. "My feeding practices are not real good," she says, so she uses granular fertilizer that will release slowly over months.

Left, Norma Boyer on the back steps through her garden. Above right, mazus reptans, a hardy ground cover.

Trials and Errors

Norma says there's nothing particularly different in her garden. "If it does well in my yard I plant more of it, because I've had a lot of failures," she says. She experiments to see what works in a sloping yard with little sun, and she doesn't fall victim to discouragement. For example, she has tried a number of clematises, and still does, even though sometimes they bloom and sometimes they don't. After her wisteria went 10 years without blooming she cut it down — but plans to try a new one from her brother's house.

Very seldom does a plant just up and die. More often it needs a new location. "Moving is great," Norma says. "I keep trying things." That gives her some unexpected successes, too, such as her daylilies — they should have full sun but hers don't because she has no full-sun area. And, as it turns out, that's fine by her daylilies.

Favorites

Pulmonaria (lungwort). It's a nice accent plant in the shade, plus it's hardy and easy, like hostas. It blooms very early with small blossoms that change color.

Columbine. It does well in the shade here and self-propagates like crazy. "Once you have it, it's everywhere," Norma says. It's easy to share with friends, and if you still have too much just rip it out. It will be back.

Right, columbine. Above, pulmonaria with red dianthus behind it.

Forget-me-nots. Although often sold as an annual, it self-seeds readily. It works for cut flowers, too.

Annabelle hydrangea. It has huge white blooms that almost glow in the evening. Norma cuts them for bouquets and gives them away. When the bush is done in the fall, she cuts it back to about a foot.

Astilbe. It does well enough in the shade that you can even use it as a ground cover in some areas.

Tips

Go on a tour. Garden tours are great for finding new ideas; Norma and her friends go as often as they can. That's where she got the idea for the drawn drapes in her outdoor room. They're just canvas drop cloths that she can toss in the washing machine in the fall.

Take photos for therapy. It's easy to get discouraged with gardening as you go along, especially in the severe Kansas City climate, so it helps to remember how far you've already come. Take photos of your garden as you're getting started and look back at them whenever your hope wanes. "You need to appreciate what you've done," Norma says.

She keeps her "before" photos in a book that shows a plain back yard with a few bushes and a concrete patch off to the side. A photo book also is helpful when it's past bloom time and you want to share a flower with a friend but need help showing what it will look like.

Visit garage sales. You can find inexpensive and interesting vases there. Buy them, stick flowers from your garden in them and give them away as special gifts.

Below, a primrose, 'Sundrops. 'Left, a 'Belle of Woking' clematis.

The Movable Garden

"It's a constant re-doing as your skills and tastes improve."

Fong Christenson
Lenexa, Kansas

ard to believe, but Fong Christenson didn't garden until 1993. When she and her husband, Craig, moved into their home in 1989, the landscape needed a major renovation. Craig went to work on the trees and shrubs, which remain his specialty. Fong, a nurse, began the flowers later with nine hybrid tea roses in one bed. "I wanted a rose garden," she says. "That's how we all get started." She began reading and searching for answers from any book she could get her hands on. "I'm a transplant myself and I knew nothing about this climate," says Fong, who is from Indonesia. Now she does — she became a Master Gardener in 1997 — and her gardens have grown and transformed. As for those original roses, you won't find them and you wouldn't recognize where they once grew.

Gaillardia 'Goblin' in the front garden provides cheerful orange tones, a color that doesn't scare Fong Christenson. Above, hollyhocks, scabiosa and a daylily decorate a birdbath.

39

Design

Fong focuses her design on shape, texture and color harmony. Some gardeners may disdain orange, but not Fong, who loves all colors. She uses silver, blue and chartreuse as neutral colors. "I'm trying to create a vignette in each area," she says. It's important, too, to build continual color by combining plants with different bloom periods. She also adds shrubs, small trees and ornamental grasses in each section to keep the garden from looking bare in the winter. Fong describes gardening as a mix of art and technique.

Renovate

You get the feeling that a shovel may be Fong's most important garden tool. Plants are continually moving around in her garden as she finds the best location for them. "You learn and redo," she says. Over time she has come to understand the micro-climates of her garden. For example, she successfully grows calla lilies by covering the bulbs with semi-evergreen ground cover and placing them next to her driveway and sidewalk for additional heat.

Left, Bergarten sage along the front walk (lower left) provided seasoning for a Thanksgiving turkey. Burberry bushes flank the steps. Above right, an asiatic lily.

Basics

Mulch. Fong relies on shredded leaves, even getting some from neighbors. But you don't see a lot of ground in her garden. She plants her flowers close enough so the leaves barely touch, which keeps the root zone cool. "The goal is living mulch," she says.

Compost. Make your own and use it. "Even if you don't dig it in, you'll be amazed what it does for your soil," Fong says. Compost feeds the soil and the worms and microroganisms in it, creating a sort of sub-soil ecosystem that in turn feeds the plants. Fong generally adds compost to the soil in the fall to take advantage of winter's thawing and freezing, which tills the ground naturally.

Some Favorites

Salvia. Especially salvia x superba 'May Night.' Salvias are perennials that come in many varieties, colors and sizes, and they do well in summer heat. After they're done blooming in early summer, cut the flowers down to the base of growth and they will bloom again in fall. Another favorite is salvia greggii ('Wild Thing').

Gaura. A hardy perennial that has a tall wispy flower you can see through. Put it in the front of the garden despite its height or it will get lost in the back.

Russian Sage. A sun-loving perennial that's easy to grow and very drought-tolerant. 'Longin' and 'Filigrin' are great, more compact varieties.

Ex-favorite

Hybrid tea roses. Fong was once up to 70 of them before she began taking them out because of the work they require to thrive. "It depends 100 percent on the gardener," she says. She still has a few but now recommends shrub roses, which bloom perpetually and better resist disease. She has more than a dozen. Her favorites include 'Knockout,' 'Carefree Beauty,' 'Morden Sunrise' and 'Evelyn,' a David Austin rose that is kind of touchy but worth growing.

Right, an asiatic lily, 'Red Emperor.' Far right, purple coneflowers, echinacea 'Magnus.'

Tips

Color. Unsure where a plant would look best? Nip off a flower and walk it around the garden until you find the best color combination.

Digging. It's better to dig your planting holes shallow and wide instead of deep and narrow, which can create a girdle that keeps roots from expanding.

Shasta daisies and mums. The key is to divide them every year, or at least every other year. The Silver Princess daisy does well in this area, especially with afternoon shade.

Must-have book. A great reference for Kansas City gardeners is *The Well-Tended Perennial Garden* by Tracy Disabato-Aust, published in 1998 by Timber Press.

Your own book. Fong keeps a 3-inch-thick notebook to help her plan her garden. She includes photos from catalogs of flowers and accessories she'd like to try, keeps notes and photos from her garden to remember successes and disasters, and saves labels from roses and other plants.

Above, asclepias tuberosa (butterfly weed) is the orange flower, and coreopsis is the yellow. Left, Fong Christenson in her garden in front of pink hollyhocks.

"I've always handled it like you would approach a piece of sculpture or a painting."

Jim Fitterling
Kansas City, Missouri

Jim Fitterling was raised on a farm near Warrensburg, Mo. He and his sister always got leftover seed packets so they had their own gardens. He went on to be an elementary art teacher for 30 years, retiring seven years ago. He's had his garden, hidden behind an apartment building in Westport, for 20 years. Jim started with zinnias and then began visiting other gardens and getting ideas. Now his garden has been on five garden tours, helping to raise $25,000 toward garden charities. The first reaction many people have on their first visit: "This garden is in this area?" It's hard to remember you're in the city until you glance around at brick buildings and overhead at power and phone lines. "I have more wires than Barnum & Bailey," says Jim, a former board member of the Garden Center Association of Kansas City.

An asiatic lily called 'Mentom'.   Above, TC the cat relaxes with pots of seed begonias.

World in a Back Yard

The sign at the entrance to Jim's garden reads, "Heaven is under our feet as well as over our heads." And Jim condenses a lot of heaven into a small space. On one side is a three-year-old pond bathed in shade. A terraced path picks its way through tall plantings behind it. Hostas fill in much of the space, while surprises include Japanese painted ferns and a jack-in-the-pulpit hiding off the path. In the center of the garden and along the back are sun beds with campanellas, poppies and a lot of color. Several antique iron urns with baskets built on top give added height to the garden, including one huge piece that Jim bought instead of taking a vacation one winter.

Jim Fitterling with his center garden in a Westport back yard. He designs his garden as he would a sculpture or painting.

Philosophy

With an artist's eye and little space to waste, Jim plans every part of his garden. He describes it as a blend of the abundant plantings of an English garden — plants crowd in so tightly you seldom see the ground — with the structure of a French garden. The center garden, with a chaos of blooms, is contained within a tightly trimmed, geometric border of boxwoods. "Structure is really more important than blooms," he says.

While he packs plants together, preferring to see plants instead of mulch, Jim says it takes extra effort to maintain the garden that way. He also plans the garden so it will bloom sequentially, starting with 400 daffodils in the spring, followed by 400 tulips and pansies, then iris, and finally all the rest in June, his peak month, which he calls his "high holy days." But even afterward, the garden looks good because of shrubs and other foliage. "I've always handled it like you would approach a piece of sculpture or a painting," he says.

Problem Plants

Gardening in Kansas City isn't easy. "We have our own set of rules," Jim says. "We're still part of the prairie."
Heat governs everything in the garden, where some plants can be difficult:

Clematis. Although he loves them, some years they're great and other years not. "They constantly deal me a fit but I won't give up," Jim says. He's found they do best if planted with a west-east exposure. Jackmanii, a traditional type, works best for him.

Veronica and roses. The five to six hours of sun a day in the garden aren't enough for them, so they're gone. "You really have to perform well in this garden or you don't hang around," Jim says.

Below, Jim Fitterling under an arbor of old-fashioned honeysuckle at the entrance to his garden. Left, A 'Blazing Sun' asiatic lily.

Tips

Pick plants for the way they look, not their pedigree. "I'd rather have something that adds to the overall effect of the garden than an unusual piece that adds little," Jim says. As a result, he doesn't shy away from common annuals and biennials, such as zinnias and hollyhocks. He even grows berbascum mullein, a tall plant that thrives in the wild and along roads, which is where he got his.

Plant the easy way. In the fall he plants larkspur and poppy seeds by simply scattering them at random, the way nature would reseed. That way they come up early in the spring.

Below, a Japanese painted fern graces the shade near Jim Fitterling's pond. Left, a Shirley poppy.

Buy plants wherever you can. That includes hardware stores and supercenters. Although nurseries have great plants, gardening can be expensive, so it's necessary to hold down costs. One August, Wal-Mart was selling half-priced boxwoods, so Jim drove from store to store, buying all he could find until he had as many as he needed.

Make your own compost. It will have more nutrients than store-bought. Jim starts in the fall with seven large trash bags of leaves, a large bag of peat moss and a cubic yard of compost. He sprinkles it with 13-13-13 fertilizer and water, and mixes it all. Jim turns it two or three times during the winter and adds more water to keep it damp.

Bridges and Bunnies

"The less work, the better."

Janice Korchak
Countryside, Kansas

The first thing you notice is the big red bridge, arcing up into the sky. It's the last place you're expecting to see a big red bridge. Janice and Tom Korchak, her husband, built it to reach an area across the creek that runs through their yard. That plot is much wilder, with wildflowers and vines, than the well-kept back yard that the Korchaks first saw 42 years ago. Janice tended the irises and hostas already there until a friend got her into the master gardening program in the 1980s. Now 80, Janice is a Master Gardener emeritus, but in the meantime she's enlarged the garden, redesigned it — and built that wonderful bridge.

Janice and Tom Korchak with the arched bridge they built from their gardens to a wilder area.
Above, a red blackberry that first began growing in that area across a creek.

Rabbit Wars

Many gardeners battle rabbits, few successfully. Janice didn't even think about rabbits, despite her rustic back yard setting, until one recent year when her neighbor's cat died. That was when she realized how useful a cat can be — she quickly was overrun with rabbits. They ate everything, larkspur and all. Janice put 30 cages around her plants but she couldn't cage everything, and the rabbits had the edge. She heard human hair might ward them off, and she had a good supply from her daughter, a hairdresser. It didn't. Then another daughter gave her two cats in early 2003. The rabbits hightailed it, the cages all came off, and Janice figures that pretty much proved the cat theory. And if you can't stand the thought of keeping a cat, try talking your neighbor into getting one.

Above, the Korchaks tend the sunniest part of their garden. Right, the cage around this foxglove has since come down, now that the rabbit problem is under control.

Garden Strategies

Janice describes her back yard as a wild, mostly shady garden that still tries to be a sun garden in some areas. While she works hard to maintain the garden, she also appreciates plants that reduce the work. She treasures a row of immense hostas she got from a friend; they don't require much meddling. Wild ginger with cup-shaped leaves spreads quickly and provides plenty of shade ground cover near the house. A shrub rose with plenty of blooms pretty much takes care of itself, Janice says. She doesn't like spraying or fertilizing — she simply tosses 5-10-5 fertilizer on everything in the spring and a month or two later. "I'm very old-fashioned," she says. "I don't keep up with all the new things in gardening, I'm sure." As for the wild area across the bridge, it's become wilder as Janice has cut back on her gardening, although she did plant a gooseberry bush she got from a friend. It gave her enough berries for three pies last year.

Left, wild blue bells that Janice Korchak didn't need to plant — they just arrived, perhaps delivered by some of the birds that live in the houses below, in the wilder portion of her property.

Tips

Move your plants. At first, Janice says, "I was loath to dig up stuff and start over." But sometimes you have to, she learned. Her red bees balm was suffering until she moved it to a location with a little more sun, and now it's thriving. The shrub rose was moved to three locations before it thrived. Besides, digging up plants gives you a chance to add organic matter and improve the soil. "It's difficult to get your soil in good shape unless you do that," she says.

Enjoy the shade. Not that Janice has much choice, with mature trees over much of the property cutting direct sun to just four to six hours in the brightest parts of the garden. But she's found that shade is good for more than just hostas. Many plants that are supposedly full sun can take part shade, she's found. For many years she gave up on delphiniums because they withered in Kansas City heat, but now she's tried again, and the magnificent blue flower does very well with some shade.

Don't get discouraged. Everyone is going to have some failures in Kansas City. Our area is regarded as one of the most difficult places to grow plants in the entire country because of extreme and abrupt weather changes, Janice says. In addition, it's on the border for plants that do better farther south, tempting us to try flowers that don't work — at least not the first time or in the first location.

Left, Janice Korchak. Above, a Stokes aster, which blooms early to mid-summer. Right, a shrub rose.

"Here's what an old man does in a new garden to make it easy."

Bob Mabes
Lenexa, Kansas

Walk around Bob Mabes' house, gawk at the garden and try to convince yourself it's only a couple of years old. It's not easy — one yarrow alone is over 5 feet tall. But when Bob, 80, moved from Prairie Village to a smaller retirement home, he brought no plants with him and didn't start the new garden until 2001. Today, thanks to his encyclopedic experience — he is a Master Gardener — his flowers are immense and thriving. Bob has branched out in recent years, too, learning to press flowers well enough to teach many workshops in the craft. He also does flower arranging and is an accredited flower show judge.

Dianthus are among the many flowers that thrive at Bob Mabes' new home. Above, one of the cards that Bob makes by pressing flowers he grows.

Cut Those Flowers

Younger people and newer gardeners are afraid to cut flowers, Bob says. Get over it if you want to really take pleasure in all your hard work and God's handiwork. "You're not out in the garden that long," Bob says. "You need to cut some flowers and enjoy them inside." To keep the flowers fresh longer, don't cut the stems too short — a common mistake. Also, be sure to harden off the plants. Take a vase of warm water to the garden, cut the flower and strip the foliage that goes into the water. Put the stem in the vase and put it in a cool place inside for eight hours. The flowers will look good for several days.

Favorites

Among the best flowers for arranging:

Lythrum. It may be a noxious weed in Northern states, but down here it controls itself and provides beautiful color.

Coneflowers. It's easy to grow native coneflowers, which require little water or fertilizer and grow in poor soil. In fact, never fertilize the natives because they'll just get tall and spindly. Bob now grows hybrids from nurseries because they're prettier.

Others. Black-eyes susans, any other perennial with a strong stem and any rose, of course.

Left, Bob Mabes with clematis that already covers a trellis with blooms. Above, a miniature rose, 'Debut.' Far left, hollyhocks.

The Secret

Bob gladly shares his biggest secret in growing thriving plants in such a short time. It's super phosphate. Phosphorous is the middle number in fertilizer descriptions, but it leaches into soil extremely slowly and may take years to reach roots. So Bob digs his planting holes 3 inches deeper than they need to be, drops in a large pinch of super phosphate, fills in 3 inches of soil, then puts in the plant. The roots will reach down to the phosphorous and the plant will flourish.

Basics

Water. Watering from above can invite disease on foliage so soaker hoses work best. But water seldom gets all the way to the end of a soaker hose so Bob has a trick: He puts an adapter on the far end of the soaker hose, then attaches both ends in a loop to a Y attachment on a supply hose. Water will make it evenly through the soaker hose.

Soil. Kansas City clay is so heavy that you're wasting your efforts if you don't work on your soil. Replace as much of it as you can with compost, peat moss, manure and other organic matter. Check with your city to see if it grinds broken tree limbs with a chipper and just leaves the chips in a pile. Bob has pails filled with chips rescued from one of those older, composted piles. He uses it as mulch, too.

Deadheading. Sorry, but you've got to do it. A plant's whole drive is to reproduce, so if it goes to seed it will stop growing and blooming. Cut the spent blooms off those flowers.

Above, pink wave petunias brighten the narrow garden in front of Bob Mabes' new home. Right, German statis blooms in the foreground of this bend of Bob's border garden.

Other Tips

Mites. Insecticides don't work well to get rid of red spider mites, but a hose does. Aim a forced stream of water from a low angle up into the leaves to wash the spiders off. Apparently the experience is traumatic enough that they don't come back. But the eggs stay, so you'll need to do it again in a week or two to get the newly hatched mites off.

Mums. Have you ever noticed that your mums aren't as great the second year as the first? That's because when they come up each year after the first one, the main stem saps strength from the new shoots surrounding it. Dig the mum up, pull off the shoots with their new roots and plant them. Toss the main stem away.

Shrubs. A great one that isn't commonly used is caryoptres. It's covered with blue flowers beginning in late summer.

Drainage. Plants sometimes die because their roots rot in dampness. Bob raises his beds 8 inches using interlocking bricks, which improves the drainage.

Below, a yellow Dahlberg daisy with a backdrop of geraniums. Left, purple scaveola blooms in this annual bed.

Acres of Garden

"It was no holds barred. We got carried away."

Doug and Catherine Niedt
Kansas City, Missouri

Some people point their chairs at the television. Doug and Catherine Niedt face two easy chairs toward a large window in their second-floor living room, giving them a view out back. You would, too — at least you would if you had turned three and a half acres into an immense flower arrangement. In fact, two stories up is not high enough to see what the Niedts have done. You miss the geometry of the herb garden. The 20-foot gazebo looks like a toy from the house and you can hardly see the shrub garden at all. The first question people often have after being stunned by the vista: "How many people help you?" None. Not that the Niedts' couldn't use the help. Both are busy. Catherine is a program supervisor for Blue Valley Recreation and Doug is a classical guitarist who teaches at the University of Missouri-Kansas City Conservatory of Music and gives concerts.

An herb garden is just one of many the Niedts have planted. Above, a bee enjoys a globe of eryngium.

71

Beginnings

Here's another question: What happened? How did two busy people end up with a flower theme park instead of a back yard? You get the sense the Niedts are working too hard on the garden to dwell much on the answer, but the outlines are clear. Doug's grandparents had a farm outside St. Louis, where they gave him a little area and let him grow some corn. He was impressed when it actually came up. In his 20s, he got some books on English country houses and noticed they usually had wonderful gardens. That started him thinking. Catherine did vegetable gardening at a university community plot in California, and Doug later introduced her to flowers. Then they moved into their south Kansas City house in 1989 and saw acres of open pasture.

Above, emilia flowers rise on long, airy stalks.

Design

They went to work first on the two flower beds behind the house. The tons of rock they dug up went into a wall for a huge croquet court off to the side. "The croquet court was the solution to the rock problem," Doug says. An herb garden went in on the other side to balance the croquet court...well, you get the idea. Now they start 4,000 annuals and herbs in their basement — so many that by August they've forgotten where they planted some of them. But nothing happens by accident. All the gardens fit into an overall design scheme that Doug describes as the packed color of an English garden laid out with the formality of a French garden.

Tips

Don't plant too early, the Niedts say. "Don't be too anxious when that first warm day of spring comes and you see all the plants in the nursery," Catherine says. "We've learned to wait until May." Last year, in fact, a busy schedule meant they were still planting by July 4th, and the garden still looked great.

Shop smart. A lot of times plants are marked as appropriate for this zone but they're not because of Kansas City's heat or humidity. Quality garden centers have people who can give you advice, Catherine says.

Do your own research, too. The Niedts have an entire bookcase filled with garden books. Another excellent resource, especially for beginners, is *Garden Gate* magazine, they say.

Below, red cleome.

Favorites

Emilia. A self-seeding annual with long stems and orange-red flowers that seem to float in the air.

Eryngium. A perennial with stunning blue globes on foliage that looks a little weedy.

Verbena bonariensis. Another self-seeding annual that the Niedts saw at Mackinac Island in Michigan. It has long stems with purple flowers.

Datura. A self-seeding annual with huge flowers that look like hibiscus. Its colors include white and yellow, blooming at dusk and lighting up the evening garden.

Cleome. It's an old annual that isn't used much here but seeds prodigiously and provides lots of color, including whites, pinks and reds.

Arctotis. A tall, white annual that can be a little finicky. It died out in some locations where they tried it, but it does well in the shrub garden.

Hydrangea Annabelle. A perennial that grows well here with large, white flowers. Don't put hydrangeas in full sun in this climate, though, the Niedts say. They work best in filtered sun for part of the day and full sun for the rest.

Knockout, a shrub rose. "This is a fabulous rose that anyone can grow in Kansas City," Catherine says.

Above, Doug and Catherine Niedt in front of one of the two mixed border gardens. Left, snow on the mountain.

A Garden Tour

The Niedts' gardens include:

Mixed border gardens. These are the first gardens that greet a visitor, bracketing the yard on the sides. They're a mix of perennials, annuals and ornamental grasses. Something is always blooming brightly, which requires a good portion of annuals. "For intensive bloom in August, you need annuals," Doug says. The flowers are packed deep and dense, which makes them a little harder to get into to work, but there's another benefit to the English look besides color. "By planting tight like that, it doesn't leave much room for weeds," Doug says.

Herb garden. With basil, sage, rosemary, chives, thyme and other herbs, it smells just as good as you'd expect. This is one of the more formal gardens, with a sundial in the middle and borders edged with winter savory, which the Niedts found is hardier in this climate than boxwood, although it requires a lot of trimming. They grew the short hedges by seeding. On one arbor is a silver fleece vine, a huge perennial that the Niedts tried after tiring of planting annual vines.

Croquet court. This technically isn't a garden, but it's very cool anyway and the overall look adds to the formality of the design. The half-size regulation court is complete with golf-green grass, providing a perfect playing surface.

The view of a few of the gardens from the Niedts' house.

Shrub garden. This one is on a slope hidden off to one side with four large, contoured beds containing flowering shrubs, conifers, yuccas and leftover annuals, providing many heights and textures. "A lot of people prefer this garden to all the others," Doug says. It's easy to see why. You can lose yourself on the wandering paths, with no buildings or other signs of the city in sight.

Knot garden. Different types of plants with similar looks are clipped to make contrasting patterns that look woven, all in tones of gray and green. At this point, it's still small while the Niedts test varieties of boxwoods and other plants to see which make it through winter. Eventually they plan to expand it to the size of the croquet court, but it will be a huge project. "Nothing is ever easy," Catherine says.

Turf maze. Again, this isn't technically a garden, but it's part of the overall design. The Niedts cut paths into the grass to make a circular maze. People on garden tours find it hard to resist testing whether they can find their way to the center.

Gazebo. Doug built this almost entirely by himself at the back of the lot, and its height of about 20 feet is surprising after catching a first, far glimpse of it from the house. Once summer activities begin winding down in August, the Niedts bring food down in a golf cart for a peaceful dinner. The gazebo is surrounded by a flower bed that used to be pasture. The Niedts never amended the soil. "It's pretty unconventional by gardening rules," Doug says. But with water and a few shots of Miracle Gro, hundreds of annuals do just fine, including castor beans with their strange colors and shapes.

Woodland garden. This is another necessary element in an English garden, so Doug cut a path with a chain saw into a wooded area. The Niedts found so much rock that they decided to leave a lot of the native plants alongside the path. Hostas and ground covers help fill in, and daffodils and other early flowers pop up in the spring. Several bridges lead into wilder areas.

Orchard. Doug planted a number of fruit trees in one area near the knot garden and works to keep the deer out of it.

Preview of coming attractions. The Niedts daydream about a new project — a garden surrounded by a tall wall, which would give it a cloistered effect. But the main purpose would be to keep out the deer and let the Niedts grow such deer delicacies as lilies, daylilies and iris. This garden hasn't yet reached the drawing board, though.

The Secret Garden

"The kids love it back here.."

Joyce North
Overland Park, Kansas

When you hear Joyce North has a secret garden, it sounds like a cute idea borrowed from a favorite childhood book. You look for it as you wander around her back yard. Maybe the secret garden is that shady corner of flowers over there, or maybe it's that quiet walkway along the side of the house. Suddenly Joyce opens a gate you hadn't seen and you look through it for an instant of pure surprise that we'll deal with in a moment. First, though, a little about Joyce. She's a retired learning specialist for a school district but still works as an educational consultant. In 1994 she became a Master Gardener, and now heads up a junior master gardener program at Horizon Academy with 14 other volunteers to help. "The kids are having a great time and I think they'll learn a lot," she says. Her husband, Bill, is a lawyer who also is retired but stays involved at his office. He's the garden digger.

A walk toward the patio, where the secret garden remains concealed. Above, begonias in one of the unusual settings Joyce North uses.

Keeping a Secret

The secret garden is a relatively new addition to the house, where the Norths have lived 35 years. In fact, it happened almost by accident. When the Norths added onto the house 13 years ago, one thing led to another and they found they had a strip of about 10 feet along the back of the lot. It was below the rest of the terraced yard and they came up with an idea — put a fence in front of it and hide it. Now, even if you knew it was there, it would be hard to find your way to it unless Joyce showed you. And once the gate swings open, you find yourself in another world — one reason the grandchildren like it so much. Impatiens add color to the long, shady garden, while other touches add whimsy. Hand-built birdhouses hang on the fence like pictures on a wall, while two truck hubcaps catch some glint of light through the trees. A parade of concrete turtles, most received as gifts, march alongside the path. An old bell from the schoolhouse in Wyaconda, Mo. — Bill's hometown — looks ready to ring.

Design

The rest of the lot has enough allure to stand as its own attraction. The back yard is all garden — don't bother to look for grass — and it feels like a huge outdoor shade room. It was all designed by a landscape architect whose detailed drawings still hang in the kitchen. The back turned into a two-level brick patio designed in concentric circles with plenty of plant beds under huge trees. Joyce uses a lot of hostas and she doesn't avoid such common flowers as begonias and impatiens. "There's not a lot of choice for color in the shade," she says. This year, in fact, she planted 30 flats of impatiens and begonias, working in a lot of pastel shades of purple, pink and white. She even shows off some of them in birdcages and other eye-catching settings. Another focus is a pond inside a round, raised brick wall where 40 goldfish, many 12 years old, watch as you pass by. "The fish pond we love," Joyce says. "It would be the last to go if we had to get rid of everything."

Above, the circle pond. Left, the secret garden, hidden behind a fence.

Favorites

Hostas. "If you have a lot of shade, you have to like hostas," Joyce says. She starts hers with some time-release fertilizer in the hole, then leaves them alone. In about three years she divides them.

Porcelain berry. This vine works in the shade and helps cover an arbor on the patio. It produces China blue berries that turn deep purple in the fall. "You can't kill it," Joyce says. Be careful, though, because it can become invasive.

Lariope. This is a type of grass that has purple flowers in spring. It fills in as shade ground cover but also tolerates some sun. Joyce cuts it down to the ground in the spring so it can restart.

William Baffin rose. This climbing rose thrives in Joyce's only sunny spot. It's only three years old but is already 12 feet tall — and would be taller if she didn't cut it back.

Below left, Joyce North. Above, begonias, impatiens and hostas thrive in the patio shade. Above left, impatiens in their own house.

Tips

Work the soil. "If you don't have good soil, nothing will do well," Joyce says. For years the Norths brought in 1,800 pounds of organic material a year to dig into the soil until it improved. Now she still mulches every year with Soil Pep, which is fine and dark.

Read the labels. You need to know what a plant will do before you fall in love with it and bring it home. "Everything looks wonderful at the nursery," Joyce says.

Start smart. For new gardens, go slowly so you don't get overwhelmed. Shrubs are a good beginning. "Then take pictures of the yard in winter so you can see what you really have," Joyce says.

Clip your hydrangeas. Joyce sometimes dries the huge white blooms from her hydrangeas, sprays them gold and uses them on the mantel at Christmas.

A huge hibiscus blooms alongside a stand of lythrum in the sun garden.

Trellises and Arbors

"This wasn't all done in one year, I guarantee you."

Connie and Jake Pflug
Kansas City, Missouri

Only eight years ago Jake and Connie Pflug looked out their back windows and saw a couple of trees standing lonely in a huge back yard. Today, they share summer evenings on a wooden patio, enjoying the frogs jumping in two ponds as flowering vines climb a half-dozen arbors and trellises. But don't be intimidated. "You have to be retired to have a garden this size," Jake says. Indeed, he's retired from the airline industry and Connie used to be a schoolteacher. She learned a lot about gardening when she took a break from teaching to run a greenhouse that the couple owned for a couple of years, and that's when Jake got interested. He's still impressed with her skill. "This yard is alive with blooms throughout the season," Jake says.

Wisteria grows heavy on an arbor the Pflugs built for it. Above, a 'Monch' aster that blooms all summer.

The Plan

The Pflugs started with a plan. They used lots of grid paper to map out the back yard before they turned their first shovel of dirt. The initial project: Dig two ponds, one bigger than the other. "We wanted them to be the focal point," Jake says. The entire garden may seem huge now, but it helps to know it happened step by step — and it's not done yet. "Even if you can't do it all at one time, you have a direction," Connie says. "Now I'm starting to work on the back 40."

Right, Connie and Jake Pflug. Above, one of the two ponds the Pflugs designed, surrounded by flowers.

Diversify

Actually, the Pflugs have more than one garden, and a visitor will find some surprise in almost every corner.
Besides the central ponds and patio, the yard includes:

A shade garden. In a small area on the side of the house is a hidden brick patio with lots of leaf cover and shade plants. Connie and Jake often enjoy mornings and evenings in the quiet seclusion of this area.

Above, gooseneck loosestrife, which can be highly invasive. Right, decorative gourds hang from a wisteria arbor. Far right, an arbor frames a corner of a pond.

An antique garden. Out in Connie's "back 40" is a tiny plot that looks almost like a pioneer garden, with a white picket fence fronting it. The flowers are almost all roses, and accessories include an antique lighting rod, old posts from a wooden porch, and the head and foot of a brass bed that their daughter rescued from a throw-away pile.

A shady fence. On one side of the yard are 50 feet of hostas in a raised bed, shaded under 14 globe locust trees. "I figured we should try something under the trees that required little work," Connie says, and hostas filled the bill. The globe locusts require annual trimming and spraying for bores, but they provide shade that's almost sculpted.

Fine Vines

Blooming clematis climb trellises in several locations in the garden while wisteria weighs down two huge arbors Jake built. Both vines regularly give other gardeners fits. The Pflugs say they have no secrets, but they do have a few tips:

Clematis. Connie says her clematis always bloom and never succumb to wilt. "I just water them and cut them down," she says. Although opinions differ on this, she cuts each clematis back to about a foot high in the fall. Each spring new growth explodes. The clematis are planted where the vines get sunshine but the roots are in shade from other plants. Each fall Connie puts cotton burr mulch around them. She recommends the old purple jacomanii as a reliable variety to start with if you want to give clematis a try.

Wisteria. The Pflugs' wisteria blooms each spring. Really. And they planted it just seven years ago from pots. Jake says you have to be careful not to trim wisteria back in late summer or fall because you'll shear off next year's blossoms. But it's a temptation to trim then because you need to cut constantly to keep the fast-growing vine under control. And it's so heavy that it will ruin a normal arbor. Jake built two heavy arbors that are set in cement, away from other plants — and still the wisteria reaches to grow up into nearby trees. "Wisteria is something that you have to work at," Jake says.

Tips

Mulch. Connie digs in as much cotton burr compost as she can in the fall in annual beds, and she spreads it over perennial beds where she can't dig. "It's made a world of difference," she says.

Thyme. It works well as a ground cover where soil conditions are bad. It stays somewhat green in the winter — and it even smells good.

Moving. Even with a master plan, Connie has moved every flower at least three times. "Most good gardeners will tell you they move plants," she says. What does well in another garden doesn't necessarily work the same way in yours, Jake adds.

Buying. Connie uses catalogs for ideas and information but does most of her buying locally, which is cheaper once you consider shipping costs, she says. And she'll go to home improvement centers as well as nurseries. "I'll buy plants just about anywhere," she says.

The Pflugs' antique garden, featuring a bedstead, old posts from a wooden porch and lots of roses.

"The bigger the pots, the easier they are to take care of."

Beverly Plapp
Overland Park, Kansas

You may think you have some large pots for your flowers, but Beverly Platt grows *trees* in containers, for heaven's sake. Not that she always did. She started, as many people do, with a potted geranium on her porch. Now she's trying to make the most of a small growing area in southern Overland Park, and big pots have turned into a big solution. So have small pots, hostas, flower beds and two dogs to keep a rampaging woodchuck at bay. Beverly, a former nurse, has gardened her entire life, helped by her husband, Fred. "He's my manual labor," she jokes. She became a Master Gardener in 1990, the year before she and Fred moved into their new house and she set to work on the yard. "It's my therapy," she says.

A sweet potato vine shares a large container with angelonia and Victoria Blue salvia (the taller plants in the back), verbena and white alyssum. Above, Beverly Plapp.

Design

The back of the Plapps' acre-and-a-half yard drops steeply into deep woods. An 11-foot wall of boulders provides enough of a terrace for a pool and a narrow garden that used to be sunny before the trees grew over it. "As your trees grow, your garden changes," Beverly says, and now she relies on sturdy hostas. But sun hits hard on the swimming pool, which is surrounded by flower beds and huge pots holding hibiscus, lantana and other colorful plants. "I finally have the pots I like around the pool," Beverly says. "I'm going for a tropical look." On a deck overlooking the pool, an Amur maple has thrived in a pot for more than five years, growing 6 feet tall, so Beverly is trying a fern-leaf buckthorn in a pot this year. Houseplants and potted hostas enjoy the shade of a patio under the deck.

A bee enjoys Victoria Blue salvia.

Wildlife

About that woodchuck. He used to come up from the woods and mow down the plants. He couldn't even eat them all so just left them lying chewed on the ground. "It was frustrating," Beverly says. That was before the arrival of their two dogs, an Airedale and a basset hound that went to work scaring off the woodchuck. But Winston and Bennie presented problems of their own, trampling some of the more delicate plants. The answer: hostas, which can withstand a lot of abuse. "I wouldn't give up my dogs, so the garden just has to survive," Beverly says. Besides, she finds herself moving more toward shrubs and hostas anyway because they're so much easier to maintain. "The older I've gotten, the fewer perennials I do," she says.

Above, Beverly Plapp with Bennie (left) and Winston, who helped solve her woodchuck problem.

Container Secrets

Big pots. The deeper the container, the more moisture it will retain and the deeper the roots can grow. But even big pots may need water every day in Kansas City heat. It also takes a lot of potting soil to fill large pots, but Beverly sees that as an investment.

Cheap pots. Beverly uses lots of plastic pots. They're cheaper and they work just fine, although sometimes she upgrades to thicker plastic that looks like terra cotta. She has nothing against ceramic containers, but they can crack in the winter if left outside.

Winter pots. When a nicer pot is too big to bring inside, Beverly winterizes it by making sure the soil is dry, covering the pot with a trash bag and tying the bag on so no moisture gets in. It's the freezing and thawing of damp soil that cracks pots.

Left, an Amur maple in the center pot is among the unusual plants Beverly Plapp puts in containers. Above, large containers provide a tropical backdrop for the pool. From left, scaveola, lantana and striped cannas.

Pot Perennials

Don't be afraid of using perennials in pots, Beverly says. Many can live through a winter if their containers are 20 to 25 inches deep and plants are hardy to Zone 3. For example, her coral bells come back each year — sometimes she even has to thin them — and so do hostas. The roots of some plants, like her huge striped cannas, need to be brought inside for the winter, but she leaves most out.

Favorites

Scaveola. A great container annual for hot, dry areas like Kansas City. Hers are a cascade of blue. "It will just grow and grow in big, deep pots," Beverly says.

Homestead verbena. Compared to most verbena, this variety is huge. In the ground, one plant can cover 6 feet, Beverly says, and even in a pot it spreads like crazy. When in the ground, it's a marginal perennial so it comes back after a mild winter. It also stands up to the heat better than the more common varieties. Like all verbenas, it needs to be sheared back in midsummer to encourage more blooms.

Becky daisy. This is the best Shasta daisy that Beverly has tried. It stands 4 feet tall without staking, and with deadheading it will bloom much of the summer.

Profusion White zinnia. It works well both in pots and in beds, and butterflies like it, too.

White Becky daisies are among Beverly Plapp's favorite plants. At right is lythrum.

"A lot of my friends think I'm crazy."

Peggy Reaka
Kansas City, Kansas

For 15 years, Peggy Reaka's lawn slumbered in quiet contentment. Then Peggy got an early Christmas present one September from her son, Jeff. "That's how it started," Peggy recalls. The gift was a pond kit, and her yard never knew what hit it. Now, just six years later, Peggy not only has a pond but also an arbor, walkways, outdoor room, gazebo and enough impressive flowers to land her on the water garden tour four of the last five years. And she's done it all with her own hands, with skill and speed that baffle her husband, Doug. After all, Peggy works full time as a computer operator. "I'm one of those weekend warrior-type of people," she says.

Huge lotus leaves are a focus in Peggy Reaka's pond. Above, a dragonhead obedience plant.

Master Plan

And Peggy is far from done. She's gradually building her way from the front of the house to the back. "It's still a work in progress," she says. For now, she and Doug can enjoy their morning coffee in a raised gazebo as they listen to the burble of water running beneath them. A creek running to the gazebo is fed by a whiskey barrel set-up she built. An antique pump display is part of the water flow. On the side of the house, Peggy is building a walkway past a secluded outdoor room that uses a wisteria arbor as a roof. No one taught Peggy any carpentry skills, although her father was handy and she got a lot of experience remodeling the interior of her house. One of her secrets is that she can map a project in her mind and then draw up a plan. Doug just shakes his head. He's sure Peggy told him about the gazebo, but he was still surprised to return from a trip three years ago to find Peggy and a friend had it half built.

Below, Peggy Reaka on a terrace planted with red coxcomb and begonias. Right, a vintage pump pours water into a stream alongside a pot with yellow coxcomb and daisies.

In the Garden

Flowers are still the main attraction each summer, though. Peggy, a Master Gardener, has a lot of luck with a strategy she describes as "by gosh and by golly." In other words, she takes a lot of risks to see what works, like the small red hydrangea she saw, liked and now grows successfully. Her tastes range from Missouri primrose to red hibiscus. Her favorites are her Stargazer lilies. They smell wonderful, last a long time and they're easy. In July as many as 25 are blooming at a time. "They're so pretty they look fake," she says.

Flower Flops

"Everybody thinks I can grow everything, but I can't," Peggy says. "I just try." That adventurous streak leads to a few disappointments. She was told, for example, that bougainvillea is too tropical for this area but she tried it anyway, with mysterious results. Two years ago it bloomed three times, but it hasn't flowered much since. It doesn't matter — she still brings it inside each winter and hopes for the best. She's working on wisteria, a notoriously tough vine to get blooming, so she's adding potassium to see if that will help. Or how about the time she sprinkled a fertilizer on a lot of plants and rain washed it all downhill into her pond, killing plants and fish. Peggy seldom gives up, but she does make accommodations — when volunteer strawberries crept into a flower bed, she simply picked the strawberries and ate them.

Below, Peggy Reaka enjoys one of her sitting areas by a gazebo she and a friend built. Left, Stargazer lilies. Below left, phlox.

Tips

Shop late and often. Peggy goes looking for perennials in late summer when they're marked down. She just sees what's available and buys up to 15 of them. (The guards at her office are used to baby-sitting plants she bought on the way to work.)

Make your life easier. For example, instead of digging up elephant ear bulbs each fall to take inside for the winter, Peggy makes sure she plants some of them in pots that can simply be wheeled inside. And she uses a trick to avoid picking up tall grasses after cutting them down. She ties a rope around the middle of her fountain grass, then cuts near the ground so she has a ready-made bale of grass to haul away.

Don't divide that fountain grass, by the way. Peggy has three tall, thriving clumps of fountain grass. Like many ornamental grasses, it often dies out in the center of the clump, but instead of dividing it, Peggy just pulls the dead branches out of the center. The plant fills itself back in.

Chrysanthemums, which Peggy Reaka lets bloom in the summer.

"The first thing you do is plan."

Rose Roos
Kansas City, Missouri

As Rose Roos walks across her back yard, a monarch suddenly flits past her eyes. "Hi, there!" she says. Butterflies are like old friends to Rose, and it's no wonder they feel welcome. Almost everything in her gardens is designed to make them happy. Moments after the monarch fly-by, several painted ladies and a bright yellow sulphur arrive and head straight for their favorite flowers. This is the sight Rose enjoys most, and she wishes she had more time to just sit on her stone patio and watch the butterflies and hummingbirds drift about, sampling this year's vintage nectar, but she's busy with family and work, too. Her husband, Phil, is a chauffeur who helps in the garden, and Rose tests software for the U.S. Department of Agriculture.

A painted lady butterfly visits a miniature butterfly bush in the back yard.
Above, Rose Roos even wears a butterfly bracelet.

Left, Rose Roos with one of her bougainvilleas.

Right, her butterfly bushes are a magnet for monarchs and other butterflies, including this painted lady.

Butterfly Essentials

Rose got interested in butterfly gardening from one of the classes she took to become a Master Gardener in 1994. She says it requires a lot more preparation than just planting some sweet-smelling flowers. Among the pieces that go into a successful butterfly garden:

Water. "To begin with, you need a water source," Rose says. She and Phil added a fountain to their back yard.

Flowers. Almost anything that has petals and nectar will work, and Rose grows a large variety of flowers that butterflies like, including coneflowers, black-eyed susans, salvia, hibiscus and petunias. Among the best butterfly attractions, though, are her four butterfly bushes. Their name is no accident, and you can find butterflies lighting there almost anytime. And don't ignore everyday marigolds, such as the ones that line Rose's front walk. "Monarchs love marigolds," Rose says.

Colors. Butterflies have limited vision, so the more colors the better, Rose says. They like both pastels and brighter flowers.

Host plants. You need these to give butterflies a place to lay their eggs and a plant for caterpillars to eat. Butterfly weed, fennel, parsley and pussy willows are among the options. And be sure to offer more than one host plant. "I learned that the hard way," Rose says. One year she had just one fennel, and it got so loaded with caterpillars that they ate the whole thing. Last year she had five fennels plus four butterfly weeds.

Basking rock. Butterflies get their energy from sunlight, so they need a place to rest and warm up in the sun.

One last caution. If you want butterflies, you can't use any pesticides in your garden.

Butterflies and Hummers

One added benefit to gardening for butterflies — hummingbirds, which love nectar too. Rose has so many of them that sometimes they scuffle to get at the two feeders she's hung in her yard. Like butterflies, hummingbirds migrate, so late summer is a good time to watch for them. "I've had a family of seven come through here in September," Rose says.

As for butterflies, the action starts by early June, when they begin arriving. In September, they're heading south. Among the varieties Rose hosts in her garden: fritillaries, swallowtails, monarchs and buckeyes.

Favorite Flower

That's easy. It's the deep red hibiscus that stands 6 feet tall on her corner, but it wasn't always so stunning.

The first two years Rose owned it, she had it in a pot and took it inside for the winter. After all, it's a tropical plant. But by the third year it wasn't looking very healthy. At the same time, she and Phil had a sunny street corner with a fire hydrant that needed some dressing up. They came up with a plan that tied in the color of the hydrant — move the hibiscus.

They planted it on the corner, with lilies and barberry bushes, and the next year it grew enormous. Because it's a hardy variety, they're leaving it in the ground over the winter and it still thrives. "It's my pride and joy," Rose says. "The trick was finding the right location." Each flower lasts only one day, but new flowers keep coming from June until the first frost.

Above, a hardy hibiscus blooms huge where Rose and Phil Roos planted it on their corner. Left, garden phlox.

Oddities

Another tropical that thrives for Rose despite living in Kansas City — two 'Rainbow Gold' bougainvilleas that she plants in pots. They bloom pink over an arbor leading to the patio in the back yard, and they're hard to miss. To keep them alive through the cold, Rose brings the pots inside each winter.

Rose also had some columbine that were doing nothing in the back, so she moved them out to the hibiscus area. Now they're huge even though they're in 90 percent sun, which can be a death sentence to columbine. Some of her hostas also flourish in the sun. "I wish I could come up with some scientific idea for why, but I can't," Rose says.

Butterfly weed, left, serves as a host plant for adult butterflies to lay eggs on in the garden. When they hatch, caterpillars will feast on the plants. Right, pots with moss roses, petunias and white geraniums brighten the back yard.

"A Master Gardener would have a heart attack to see me grow things."

Fran and Richard Semler
Kansas City, North, Missouri

Motorists who slow on Prather Road to ogle the colorful hollyhocks or check on the continuing scarecrow drama still haven't seen the best of the Semlers' garden. It starts in the front yard, winds to a stunning back yard and drops down a hillside to Prather. The garden has been growing for 15 years. Fran, inspired by a grandmother who kept a yard full of flowers, does a lot of the designing and growing. Richard does the thankless grunt work. They are members of the Clay County Rose Society and Northland Gardeners of America.

One of Fran Semler's favorite flowers, white garden heliotrope, along with one of her unusual planters. Above, a rabbit that she bribes with carrots to stay out of her flowers.

Design

Fran describes her yard as a country garden because it has flowers everywhere, and not much grass. Fish ponds are in the front and back, along with walking paths, 200 roses and many other plants. The size of the garden was probably inevitable because Fran can't stand to throw anything out. "There's not a plant I ever see that I don't like," she says. In fact, she loves rooting new plants from cuttings and has a cold frame on one side of the house just for that purpose. A back room in the house is dedicated to gardening, too. And in the middle of all that green there's even some whimsy. One year, the Semlers set boy and girl scarecrows at opposite sides of the hill garden, and over the summer they gradually moved closer until they finally met. During the next several weeks they hugged and slowly walked up the hill.

Drivers along Prather Road in Kansas City, North, can enjoy the Semlers' colorful ranks of hollyhocks, right, or follow a drama in which scarecrows slowly move about the garden over the summer. Below, the two scarecrows finally meet.

Garden Without Fear

"I don't have a problem whacking stuff down," Fran says. In fact, probably only

mobsters use the word "whack" more than Fran. Once a plant like a hollyhock is done

blooming, she'll get it out of the way by cutting it way back. She's not afraid of trying

the unconventional, such as the year she emptied her garage of different kinds of left-

over fertilizer granules and tossed them on the garden. No problem. Or how about the

slopes she gardens — one so steep she needed to lay a ladder on the ground just to

plant it. Although some friends worried the soil would wash away, it held, thanks to

ground cover, mulch and new plants taking root.

Above, instead of chopping down a dead willow, the Semlers used it to show off flowers.
Left, water lilies in a barrel, with a pump from the farm where Fran Semler grew up.

Favorites

Coleus. Sometimes even a veteran like Fran finds something new. Her coleuses, with huge and gorgeous foliage, have become a recent favorite. "I'm hooked on them," she says. She keeps hers in shade, and now each year takes cuttings to keep alive under a grow light through the winter.

Garden heliotrope. The small white flowers grow in a ball and smell like vanilla. They're done blooming by July but then re-seed themselves all over the garden. It's fairly uncommon — she found it in a seed catalog.

Roses. Although 200 may seem like an impossible number of roses to keep going, "once you develop a rhythm it's as easy to grow 200 roses as 20," Fran says. She has started using a hose sprayer for insects and disease, which makes the work easier, but she says you need to start spraying in April. Over the year, sprinkle some Epsom salts around the drip line of the rose a few times to help it through the summer, she says. And if you're really serious, join a rose club, where other gardeners are eager to help you. One persuaded Fran to go to the state fair with her roses a year ago and she won 27 ribbons.

Below, Richard and Fran Semler on their hill. Right, a 'Veterans' Honor' rose.

Tips

Don't kill yourself. Start slowly. "If you start big you'll run out of energy," Fran says. It takes a lot of work to establish a garden and control weeds in the first years. It's easier later. Fran plans to make it easier still by switching gradually to perennials, which take less work. "I'm getting this garden ready for my old age so I won't have so much to do," she says.

Water. A common mistake for new Kansas City gardeners is not watering enough. "It's hard to water too much in this climate," Fran says.

Weeds. Try tossing some pre-emergent over perennial beds in the spring. It won't hurt the perennials and it will keep weeds down. Fran's other advice: Mulch, mulch, mulch.

Chrysanthemums. They can bloom twice. At least they do for Fran. She lets mums bloom in June and then cuts them back. They'll still come back in the fall with new flowers. If you don't believe it, try it on just some of your mums and see.

Gladiolus. Here's a secret to keep them from falling over. Dig a trench for the bulbs and put them at the bottom with just a little dirt over them. As they grow, gradually fill in the trench with dirt. That will give the base of the flower much more support.

Richard and Fran Semler in their back yard sun garden, above the hill they have also turned into a huge lower bed.

Wild in the Suburbs

"I have a lot of areas where things are just duking it out."

Sheila Shinn
Blue Springs, Missouri

Walk through Sheila Shinn's gate and you find yourself in a riot of color where hundreds of plants compete in seeming chaos, threatening to overrun what little lawn remains. It's an interesting change from the careful gardening going on behind most suburban homes, but it's not as primitive as it looks. Sheila, a Master Gardener, knows exactly what she's doing, and she has for many years. Sheila began gardening as a child. In fact, she recently found a garden journal from childhood. She was inspired by a neighbor who spent a lot of time in the yard and let Sheila follow her around the flower beds. "I know now she was an obsessed gardener," says Sheila, who nonetheless caught the lifelong passion. "That's the neat thing about gardening," says Sheila, a retired social studies and English teacher. "It's a continual mystery."

Blue larkspur and red Shirley poppies brighten the "crazy quilt" garden.
Above, "The Whisperer" hides in the gardens.

Design

Bees and butterflies swoop through Sheila's garden, which is no happy accident. She gardens for wildlife. Hummingbirds love her larkspur and her patch of red monarda. Sheila makes sure something is always blooming and she tries to mimic nature by creating different levels of plants, from overhanging tree branches above to ground cover below. She also mixes in plenty of wildflowers, including Virginia bluebells and celedine poppies. She calls the most colorful area her "crazy quilt" bed, with lots of old-fashioned annuals that she lets re-seed, including Shirley poppies and nigela. She uses natural fertilizers, mixing blood meal, bone meal and green sand, but rarely needs to supplement organic matter. By the time she's done, the lot where she's lived for almost 20 years is much more garden than yard. "It's a little piece of wilderness in suburbia," Sheila says.

Above, dame's rocket. Above left, Sheila Shinn with larkspur and poppies. Left, old-fashioned yarrow that came from the garden of Sheila's mother.

Favorites

Campanula. A gorgeous flower that comes in many varieties — Sheila has 10 of them — including a lot of blue colors. It's easy to grow and seems to take difficult conditions. Although the work is tedious, if you deadhead after the first bloom, some varieties will come back soon with more and continue for much of the summer. After that, cut back the stalk and leave the foliage, Sheila says.

Dame's rocket. It spreads well by re-seeding itself, and its fragrance attracts butterflies and hummingbirds. Deadheading this Missouri wildflower also leads to a later rebloom.

Daylilies. They're easy to grow, come in a great variety and have a long bloom period. Each day brings new blooms. "I can hardly wait to get up in the morning," Sheila says. Each year she treats herself to buying a new variety.

Coreopsis. Just about anything in that broad family is wonderful. It's reliable and has good foliage, even when it's not blooming.

Failures

Even Sheila couldn't get one wildflower, a Himalayan blue poppy, to work. She was sure she could get it to grow but Kansas City is just too hot and humid. She also stopped growing gaillardia, a lavish perennial, because it never came back the next year. And she still has some penstemon, but most of hers didn't live long.

She restrains her gardener's optimism by self-imposing a three-strike rule. "If I really like it, I'll try it three times," she says. "If it still doesn't come back, I give up."

Left, a shady area gives Sheila Shinn a cool view of the back gardens. Right, Shirley poppies.

135

Tips

Pot it. Many gardeners grow lantana and caladium as annuals, but Sheila puts them in pots in the garden and brings them in for the winter. The lantana goes in the garage and loses its leaves, but it comes back in the spring and now has grown into a handsome bush. Her half-dozen caladiums all go in the basement until spring, re-emerging just as colorful as the previous year.

Write it. Sheila keeps a garden journal to aid her memory. It helps her recall what she's planted, where, and when it will emerge. That way she won't dig up a patch in April where a plant is waiting to come up in May.

Share it. Many plants are from her old home and her family. She has poppy seeds that have been in the family since the early 1800s. She remembers seeing one bromeliad she still has in her garden when she was a child, more than 50 years ago. She describes those "pass-along" plants as one of the great joys of gardening because they have become part of her heritage. As an aunt once told her: "It's so much nicer to have plants from someone else than to buy them."

Below, a "pass-along" asiatic lily. Many of Sheila Shinn's flowers came from family and friends. Left, a stone-edged pond enhances the rustic feel of the back yard.

"They grow as you go. That's the fun part."

Paul Van Lerberghe
Shawnee, Kansas

When Paul Van Lerberghe moved into his house 21 years ago, the previous owner told him the soil was terrible and Paul would never be able to grow anything. It turns out the owner was only half right — the ground is indeed terrible. But Paul regarded the rest of the prediction as a challenge and he's proved it wrong, growing hundreds of annual flowers every year. For inspiration, he reached back to Belgium, where he had lived most of his life. He grew up on a farm where his mother worked hard to grow a flower garden so lovely that people from town would walk out to see it. "I always remembered that," Paul says, and his yard is now a tribute to that memory. Paul is a wine consultant, and with his wife, Jenny (Adriana), he enjoys watching their grandchildren play in the garden. He also has hosted tours, including the Shawnee Garden Club.

Chickens add a Belgian touch to Paul Van Lerberghe's gardens, which feature annuals such as these begonias and marigolds. Above, petunias.

Left, coleus in a pot set in an impatiens bed.
Above, Paul Van Lerberghe starts out thousands of
annual seedlings each year in his greenhouse.

Paul's Plan

Paul doesn't consider himself an expert on horticulture or design. For him, flowers are far more a recreation than a skill set. "You need a hobby — if you have dead time you have to do something," he says. Yet that discounts the magnitude of Paul's gardening. Several years ago he built a greenhouse because he needed to. With all his flowers, "you can't afford to buy them all," he says. Now he starts many from seeds and grows plugs of almost 2,000 others that are harder to seed, including petunias, begonias, vinca, salvia and impatiens. It gives him a lot of joy as he watches all those flowers grow. "Once you get it going, then you go and go and go," he says.

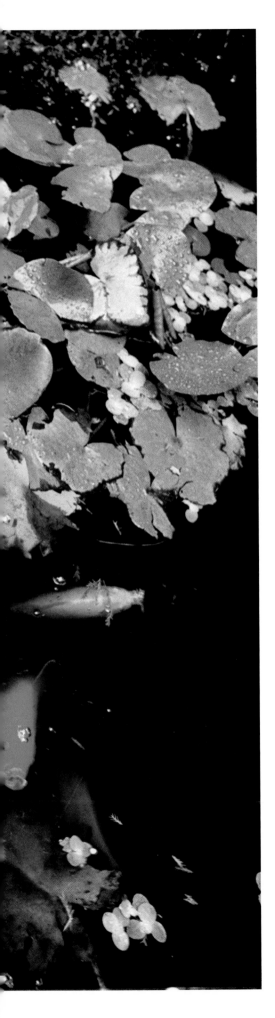

Back Yard Areas

Flower beds. Paul has several areas, ranging from a manicured bed of begonias to a much less formal rock garden that includes lots of marigolds, zinnias and coleus, all grown from seed. He lets the grandchildren play in the rock garden, and he makes sure there's not much there that they can damage.

Water pond. Paul started with a 4-foot pond and then went on a garden society tour one day. "I went home, got a shovel and started digging," he recalls. Now the pond is 2,400 gallons with a waterfall and huge goldfish. He discovered that the fish, which he bought for $1 a dozen from a bait shop, grow according to the size of the environment. Lantanas fill in the area in front of the pond, but his favorite spot is behind it, where a small bridge leads into some deep shade. "It's always cool," he says. "You can relax, bring a book, listen to the water and talk to the chickens."

Chicken house. Yes, chickens. He got the idea from Belgium, which he left in 1981 and still visits frequently. Belgians recycle a lot of kitchen waste by feeding it to chickens, cutting overall trash by up to 10 percent. "I thought, 'I'll do that!'" says Paul, and he did. He built an attractive house for six chickens, which give him up to a half-dozen eggs daily. There's an added benefit. "It's nice when you're in the back yard — they're always talking," Paul says.

Chubby goldfish enjoy the pond Paul Van Lerberghe expanded several years ago.

Tips

Feed annuals often. Paul uses Miracle Gro on the 1st, 10th and 20th of the month to make sure his flowers get some food every 10 days. With enough water and food, you can grow almost anything, he says.

Pinch your salvia. Many Americans haven't discovered the secret of annual salvia, he says. If you take off the first bloom when it appears, the salvia will get bushy with a half-dozen blooms instead of just one, lonely tall one. "But it's hard to do," he says. "In the spring you want a bloom."

Don't try to beat the spring. Paul never puts flowers outside before May 10. If you plant them sooner, a frost may kill them, and even if it doesn't, the cold nights make sure your plants don't really get a head start. "Maybe you won't kill them, but they won't develop," Paul says. "They almost go backwards."

Weed every day. That way, Paul says, "it won't get away on you."

Deadhead annuals. That's about as much fun as weeding, but it gives flowers energy to produce new blooms.

Favorites

Sunflowers. Not only are they striking, but they also attract finches. Paul avoids the tallest, one-flower varieties and goes for those with multiple blooms. "They always work," he says.

Rose of Sharons (hibiscus syriacus). These colorful bushes fill in two fence lines for Paul. They bloom from July to fall and grow up to 8 feet. They may not be used much here because they die easily, but they also self-seed. "It it dies, it dies," Paul says. "There's another one coming."

Hyacinth bean. Paul lets one grow up a 16-foot birdhouse pole each year as a centerpiece of the garden. The pink flowers turn to bright red bean pods. It's an annual, but you can save the seeds for next year.

Right, a hyacinth bean vine climbs a birdhouse pole. The flowers bloom purple.
Above left, zinnias in a bed near the pond.

Himalayan Gardening

"It certainly is homemade, but I like it."

Anne Vogelweid
Bonner Springs, Kansas

*Anne died shortly before this book was published.
This chapter reflects the skills learned by a wonderful gardener.*

Up above Lake of the Forest, Anne Vogelweid's home perches on the side of a hill with a year-round view that's hard to match in the Kansas City area. But for real sightseeing, try the narrow lot along the side of her house. The steep slope doesn't look suitable for walking, much less gardening, but it's covered with flowers and other plants. The secret: more than a half-dozen terraces that Anne put in herself over a number of years. "I was younger," said Anne, a retired teacher. "I don't know if I'd do it again." But all that work certainly didn't muffle her passion for gardening. Anne later became a Master Gardener and worked on the flower bed at the Agricultural Hall of Fame, which has now named it the Anne Vogelweid Memorial Garden.

A wild daisy grows among the baby's breath.

Design

When Anne moved into the house in 1994, the side yard was a disaster. The front was a problem, too — it was all grass. A good lawn requires herbicides, which Anne didn't like to use. She dug up the front over almost two summers and put in her first terrace. Then she cleaned out the side and terraced it with rock over the next few years. A narrow walking path on each terrace helped her get at her plants. Despite the terracing, though, the hill doesn't look landscaped. Plants aren't spaced closely together — there wouldn't be much room for that anyway — and the stone walls are more rustic than geometric.

Shade Problems

Except for the front garden, Anne's entire lot is in the shade, so she tried a lot of different plants. And, she said, "I have had many failures." She found that many plants that books say should work in the shade really need some sun. In fact, except for begonias, she never found any great flowering plants for shade.

Shade Solutions

That doesn't mean you can't have fun without the sun. Here are some of Anne's shade favorites:

Pulmonaria (lungwort). A perennial that comes in many varieties. It blooms early, before overhead leaves are out, and then has beautiful green foliage all summer.

Brunnera macrophylla (langtrees). It's got great little flowers in the spring and good foliage all summer.

Hostas. It's hard to go wrong with these workhorses. "I plant them and they grow," Anne said. Just be careful not to plant them too closely together. They'll be fine for a few years and suddenly they'll grow huge, crowding each other. Divide them, but only when you need to.

Bleeding heart and forget-me-nots. They work well in the shade but die back in the summer.

Anne Vogelweid terraced her steep hillside so she could garden on it. Above, pulmonaria, a great shade plant.

Be Careful

Two invasive plants Anne never tried again:

Trumpet vine. It grew roots underground, coming up five feet away in her garden.

Petasites japonicus (giganteus). It was actually worse than trumpet vine, emerging from the ground 10 feet away.

Below, butterfly bush, `Royal Red.'
Right, rudbeckia.
Far right, bee balm, `Cambridge Scarlet.'

Sun Favorites

Rudbeckia, purple coneflowers and bee balm. They all provide a lot of tall color in Anne's garden. Rudbeckia (black-eyes susans) makes great cut flowers, but divide it in the spring or it will clump.

Butterfly bushes. The medium purple variety is especially good at attracting butterflies, Anne said.

Goatsbeard. It looks a little like a sun garden astilbe and it's very reliable, coming back every year.

Tips to Save Work

Use ground cover instead of mulch. Anne started growing sedum and creeping jenny when she got tired of lugging bags of mulch up the hill, and both now cover a lot of area. Creeping jenny does well in the shade, but not sedum. She also acquired wild ginger — by accident. "It just showed up," she said. But it does very well in the shade, especially if it gets enough water.

Bring your pots inside each winter. Anne brought her begonias, geraniums and potted azaleas in before cold weather, keeping them alive under grow lights until they go back out in the spring. "I hate to throw anything that's growing away," she said.

Do your homework. Go to bookstores, libraries or the Internet to research plants. Learn where to plant them, how to grow them and what works well in drought and Kansas City heat. But books won't tell you everything, so you'll still need to experiment. "You learn all this stuff from books and classes, but I've found that what works for you works for you," Anne said.

Shop in late summer. That's when perennials go on sale. They'll look terrible when you plant them but they'll come up fine the next year.

Above, Beacon Silver, a good ground cover for shade. Left, Anne Vogelweid under an arbor of climbing hydrangea, with her hill behind her.

Wall-to-Wall Roses

"Rosebushes don't always do what you want them to do."

D.O. "Dink" and Margaret Watskey
Independence, Missouri

The Watskeys' roses seem impossibly tall and full from a distance. Up close they're even more impressive — full blooms, no black spot, no insect damage. None of that happened by accident. The couple started growing roses back in 1954, inspired by a neighbor. They went to a nearby rose show at a school and Dink got talked into joining the American Rose Society. Soon they were so enthralled that Dink quit smoking and put the cigarette money he saved in a box to buy new roses. By 1958 they already had won the Nicholson Bowl, the American Rose Society's top national trophy. In the years since, their rose beds grew in their back yard and they added a bed of miniature roses. And they've won so many trophies that they need to store many of them with a friend. Dink retired in 1985 as a tool and dye maker. Margaret, a medical office secretary, retired in 1987. They are members of the Jackson County Rose Society and the American Rose Society, which awarded Dink the Silver Honor Medal this year for outstanding service.

A 'Rina Hugo' hybrid tea rose. Above, an 'Honest Red.'

Getting Started

First, you need to know that there's nothing easy about rose gardening in Kansas City. It's labor-intensive, and laziness will be penalized.

Buying roses. Dink buds almost all of his onto root stock. If you need to ask what that means, you're probably not ready to try it yet.

Even though he hasn't bought any for years, Dink generally prefers bareroot. He recommends #1 bushes from reputable nurseries. Cut the tips off the roots to encourage new growth. Also, prune stems back to about 10 inches, making the cut 1/4-inch above the bud eye, slanting 45 degrees toward the back of the bud. This makes the stem grow out and keeps the center of the bush open for better air circulation. Soak the whole plant in water overnight before planting. Plant in March and then hill up 10 inches of soil around the base to protect them from freezing.

If you do buy roses already potted, buy them in May when they're blooming. If you try to plant a potted rose too early, the soil will fall away because the roots have not grown enough to hold it together. Let the dirt dry out in the pot a few days before planting, then water it about every three days for several months, depending on the weather.

When planting any roses, you should dig a hole 18 inches by 18 inches and mix additives (more on that coming up). The bottom of the bud union — the knob — should be even with the soil.

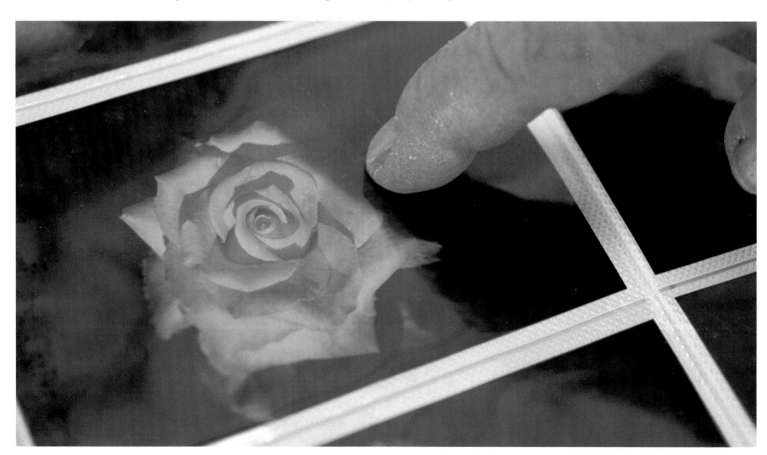

Sun and Water

Roses should get full sun, half a day at the minimum.

The Watskeys use soaker hoses about 11 hours once a week when the temperature is in the low to mid-80s. The point is to soak the soil about a foot deep. Soaker hoses work well because the entire area gets wet, and dry areas on the perimeter don't draw moisture away. "They've got to have water if they get nothing else," Dink says. "If roses don't get water, you don't get anything." When the summer gets into the 90s, you may have to water two or three times a week.

Some experts recommend mulching, but the Watskeys don't. Mulch brings feeder roots back up to the surface, they say, and it can drown roses in wet weather. Instead, as soon as the soil is dry enough, they scratch up the bed to a depth of 2 inches — that's called "dust mulch," and it makes the feeder roots go down into the soil.

Above, Dink and Margaret Watskey with an 'Elizabeth Taylor' rose. Left, Dink Watskey took a series of photos to document the blooming of a 'Touch of Class' rose.

Pruning

When cutting back a stem after a rose has bloomed, go to the first set of five leaflets, go up a 1/4-inch on the stem and cut at a 45-degree angle.

Fertilizing

The Watskeys use a mix of fertilizers to start their roses off in early May. They dig a 3-inch-deep trench around each rose, 6 to 8 inches from the bud union, and add:

 1/2 cup of Osmocote

 1 cup fish meal

 1 cup alfalfa meal

 1/4 cup Epsom salts

Fill in the trench. Water using liquid fertilizer, 1 tbs. per gallon per bush. Osmocote is slow-release pellets that last three to four months, and Dink says it doesn't work until the soil warms to 70 degrees so the liquid fertilizer gives roses a fast boost in the spring. If you like you can use liquid fertilizer at mid-month every month until mid-August.

Diseases and Bugs

To prevent black spot, the Watskeys use Banner Maxx, a water-based fungicide. It's pricey but it goes a long way and the remainder can be kept. Spray it every two weeks and be sure to get both sides of the leaves.

For bugs, Watskeys have luck using Orthene Wettable Powder every two weeks. However, watch the foliage for insects. At times you may need to spray weekly. Again, Dink says, be sure to get the underside of leaves, where 90 percent of bug activity occurs. In fact, Dink pulls off the bottom leaves of roses 6 to 8 inches above the soil to make it easier to spray under the rest of the leaves, where red spider mites reside. If left unchecked, red spider mites can defoliate a bush. They can be controlled if sprayed weekly with Avid.

'Veterans' Honor.'

Winter

How devastating can winter be? In 1992 alone, the Watskeys lost 70 bushes because a Halloween freeze hit before they were ready. But most years they seldom lose bushes — some are decades old — because they're so careful.

Their blueprint for winterizing:

- In mid- or late October, take the bottom leaves off about 2 feet up from the ground.

- Then cut out any stubs and dead canes, leaving room for new ones. "For practical purposes I do my spring pruning in the fall," Dink says.

- Pull all the branches together in a bundle with soft cotton rope and tie them with twine.

- If possible, cover the bud union with 6 inches of soil, mulch or compost.

- Cut the canes so they're about a foot and a half higher than the cone you will use.

- Put the top of the canes through the cone. Dink uses Styrofoam cones with removable lids, and boxes for bigger bushes. He uses oak leaves, shredded or whole, and packs them well.

- When the temperature will go below 20, cut the canes below the top of the cone and put the lid on with a brick to hold the cone down.

- When the temperature is above 20 for two or three days, slide the lid partly off to prevent mold and mildew.

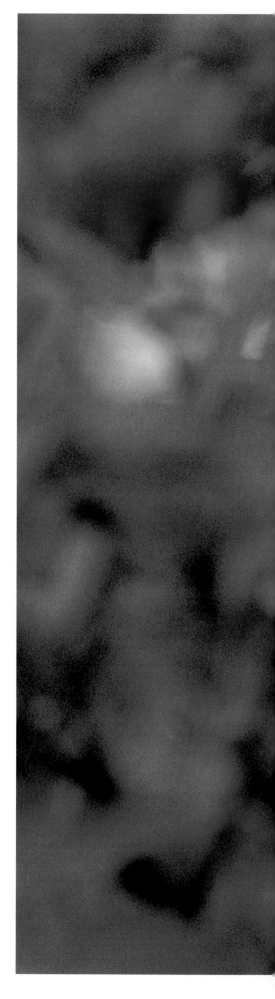

'Signature,' one of the Watskeys' favorite roses.

160

Watskey Favorites

Many of their favorite roses are older varieties and no longer available from standard locations and catalogs. Specialized nurseries might have them, though. All except the last are hybrid teas.

Veterans' Honor. A fragrant, dark red.

Louise Estes. White and pink with lots of petals.

St. Patrick. Their best yellow.

White Masterpiece. A 40-year-old bush. "Some roses work well for other people, some work well for you," says Margaret. "We think of this as our rose."

Signature. Deep pink, good form.

Uncle Joe. Dark red, 70 petals. Never opens completely because there are so many petals. This one is more common than some other favorites.

Rina Hugo. A hot pink.

Papa Meilland. Deep red. "Everyone should have it for fragrance if for nothing else," Dink says.

White Success. Blooms are excellent; not as big a bush as some others.

Elizabeth Taylor. Deep pink, prolific bloomer.

Crystalline. White, good form; originally a florist rose.

Moonstone. White with pink edges. "It blooms like crazy," Dink says.

One grandiflora: Fragrant Plum. Fragrant, mauve.

Dink's Planting Soil

Dink mixes his own soil. Here's his recipe.

Combine:

    40 pounds of top soil

    4 gallons of spagnum peat

    1 and a half gallons of perlite

    (No fertilizer)

For planting potted roses, mix all the above, then add:

    1 cup fishmeal

    Half cup Fertilome or other rose food

    1 cup alfalfa meal

    Half cup lime, if needed

Above, Dink and Margaret with 'Veterans' Honor.' Left, 'St. Patrick,' another Watskey favorite.

"There are as many ways of building ponds as there are people who want to build them."

Pat and Rodger Wright
Lee's Summit, Missouri

First you hear the burble. Then you see the stream tumbling down to a placid pond. And once you think you've taken it all in, a bullfrog hiding nearby suddenly hits the water like a basketball dropped from a tree. Water gardens are one of the hottest trends in gardening, and Pat and Rodger Wright's pond shows why. Pat, a Master Gardener, recently co-chaired the Water Garden Society of Greater Kansas City tour, which has included the Wrights' own garden three times. And yet it never gets old to them. "Listen to it," Rodger says as water runs over a rock waterfall into the pond, where a plump white fish named Herzog drifts by just under the surface.

Purple coneflowers reflect in one of the Wrights' ponds. Above, a night-blooming cereus.

Fields and Streams

The Wrights had the water garden built just seven years ago with professional design and construction help, including some muscle from a Bobcat. Although their lot has more rock in it than they'll ever use, they brought in hard rock because the native sandstone will split in a few years. Taking advantage of a natural slope, they put in an upper pond that feeds two waterfalls and two lower pools into a 50-foot stream that finally empties into the main pond. Now tall lotus flowers and water lilies bloom in the morning light with a broad paver patio for viewing. "It's a great place to entertain," Pat says. That still left them with plenty of space on their two acres — it takes three hours for a riding mower to finish the lawn. "You have to push it as fast as you can down the straightaways," Rodger says. They're gradually filling a little of it in with a bog garden, a wildflower garden and a shade garden.

So You're Thinking About It

If you're daydreaming about starting a water garden, where do you start? "Join the water garden society," says Pat. "We can provide a lot of guidance." Don't worry that the lay of your land is wrong. A water garden can go on a slope, like the one the Wrights have, or you can build your own waterfall on a flat lot. But it's important that the pond get enough light. Lilies need four to six hours of sun a day to bloom, and lotus require at least that and more. If you want to try water gardening without hiring a Bobcat, or digging the hole yourself, fill some tubs with water and grow some plants in those. Pat grows lilies, papyrus and other tropicals in containers.

Gills and Wings

Ask Pat why she loves water gardens, aside from the sound, and her answer is simple: "The wildlife and the birds." That includes two big bullfrogs that bellow like a fog horn whenever they feel like it. Herzog, a koi, and a number of shubunkins and other fish fill the pond, where they can nap beneath the ice all winter. Some fish even swim in tubs Pat fills with water for lotus and other plants, where they eat the larvae that would otherwise hatch into mosquitoes. As for birds, Pat lets a birch hang low over the stream to give them some privacy as they drink. They've even hosted a great blue heron — which, actually, is not a good thing. Herons are the Freddy Kruegers of water gardens, picking off fish one by one until none are left. But gardeners have a few defenses, including a rubber snake on the edge of the Wright ponds.

Right, a frog relaxes on a lily pad in the main pond.
Left, the main pond in the Wrights' gardens.

Above, Rodger and Pat Wright with their dogs, from left, Abby, Buffy and Darcy. Left, a lotus blooms in the pond.

Hard Lessons

Even great gardeners hit bumps. From experience, the Wrights now know:

Slope the edges of flower beds surrounding ponds away from the water. Otherwise plants can slide into the pond. And be sure there's no lawn runoff of herbicides and fertilizer into the pond. Neither fish nor plants will appreciate it.

Find someone dependable when you go on vacation to watch the water level. One year, a helper left a hose running and almost all the Wrights' fish died — tap water needs to be dechlorinated to be fish-friendly.

Don't buy any more from the nursery than you can plant in the next three days. "It's like going to the grocery store when you're hungry," Pat says.

Favorites

The Wrights do a lot of gardening in
the dirt as well as the water.
A few of their favorites:

Hawera. It's a spring bulb, short like a hyacinth but actually it's a daffodil with more than one flower per stem. Pat says you should fertilize all bulbs right after they bloom. Leave foliage until it browns and dies back so it can energize the bulb for next year.

Night-blooming cereus. A cactus that only flowers at night and each flower only lasts one night. "The red seedpod looks like a strange Christmas bulb or something from outer space," Pat says. She got hers as a stem from a friend in Phoenix and put it in a pot, where it bloomed seven years later.

Persian shield (strobilanthus). It's excellent to use as a foliage accent. When light hits it right, it seems iridescent, but it's not used in pots as much as it should be, Pat says.

Left, water lilies opening in the morning.
Right, a 'Maggie Belle Slocum' lotus thrives in a tub.

Perennial Pleasures

"It's fun to walk through a garden and see something unexpected."

Julie Zoller
Paola, Kansas

As you wander through Julie Zoller's manicured central garden, admiring the roses and other perennials, you suddenly look and wonder if you're seeing right. Is that a tomato plant? Yes, indeed. Just because a garden has a theme doesn't mean it can't have a few punchlines, too. Julie learned a lot about flowers from her mother and grandmother while growing up in Colorado, and continued gardening in Overland Park. Nine years ago, she and her family moved south to the country and began gardening in earnest on a whole lot more land. Julie, who works in real estate, gets lots of help in the garden from husband Bob, son Grant and especially daughter Jaclyn. Gardens aren't all that catch the eye — the family lives in the old Wellsville train depot, which was moved to the lot in 1988. Julie helped start a Paola garden tour that has included her gardens twice.

One of the Zollers' dogs, Dingo, on the front walk as the sun brightens the central garden in the background. Above, Lucy enjoys another part of the garden.

Gardens

Most of Julie's plants are perennials, but that's where predictability ends. "Your gardening changes because you want variety," Julie says. Perennial gardens have less color than annual displays, so she adds interest with some bright annuals, such as larkspur. She especially enjoys purple and yellow combinations. Odd sculptures, giant birdhouses and an old outhouse used as a gardening shed pick up the slack when not much is blooming. As for the tomato plant, almost anything goes in the "potage" design of the front garden, modeled on French gardens with huge variety. In addition, Julie has several shadier beds, including a woodland garden.

Clematis grows over an arbor in front of the Zollers' home.

Favorites

Acanthus mollis (with the colorful common name Bears Breeches). It has an unusual bloom in mid-July, coming up from the stem with little buds piled on each other. It likes shade and moisture but can stand a little morning sun. Mulch it in the winter.

Ligularia. Another favorite shade plant, this one is so big it will stop you in your tracks. The leaves, which have edges like knife teeth, are green on top and burgundy on the bottom, with burgundy stems and veins. It takes about an inch of water a week.

Problem Plants

None, really. Delphiniums are beautiful but don't do well in Kansas City heat and fickle winter temperatures. The longest Julie has kept one alive is four years, but it's worth the effort, she says.

In fact, Julie says, just keep trying if you don't have luck with a plant you really like. "There are always new varieties, so keep watching for them," she says. "Never give up on one you like."

Left, Julie Zoller and daughter Jaclyn, who helps with the gardening. Right, a daylily, Hemerocallis 'Stella De Oro.'

Tips

Don't ignore foliage, especially in a perennial garden. Leaf structure is important when there's not a lot of color, so Julie uses lots of variety, including plants with variegated and fern-types of foliage. Julie especially enjoys putting herbs in perennial gardens for texture.

Mulch in winter. She uses up to 2 inches of cotton-burr mulch, which can make walking in her garden a little like stepping onto a trampoline. Not only does it keep weeds down, it even lets some annuals survive the cold and pop back up in the spring.

Pamper those first-year perennials. Give them more water than normal until they get established.

Trim perennials fearlessly. Some will surprise you by reblooming. For example, cut veronica back to the first joint after it blooms and you can see another bloom coming. Salvia also will rebloom after you cut it back.

Trade perennials and let your friends save you some money. Julie sometimes has a pot luck lunch at her house so people can exchange their extra perennials after dividing them in the spring. And she never passes up a chance to pick up a new plant, once bringing a hosta back from a Michigan vacation in a suitcase.

Start new gardens with newspapers. Instead of digging up all the grass where you want to put a new garden, just dig your plants into the lawn. Then surround them with 6 to 8 layers of newspaper, laid out on the grass, and cover the newspaper with compost. You won't need chemicals to kill the grass and the newspaper will eventually decompose.

Watch the sun. If an area gets more than five hours of sun a day, look for plants with high drought resistance. You'll still have to water at least every other day in high sun areas, and early watering in the morning works best.

Above, a hidden shade garden highlighted by an English birdhouse. Left, delphinium. It's beautiful, but it takes some work to keep growing in Kansas City weather.

Flowers for Kansas City Summers

It's August in Kansas City. The rain stopped a month ago. The temperature tops 90 every day, and 100 on many of them. The soil — never that great to begin with — bakes. And all over the city, flowers give up the struggle.

Even the best gardeners sometimes feel like wilting, too. But professionals can't. They need to keep their flower beds looking good from spring through fall because visitors don't stop coming.

How do they do it? Here a couple of experts share some tips for ways both you and your garden can survive August in this climate.

A purple coneflower (echinacea purpurea 'Magnus'). Above, garden phlox.

Welcome to Kansas City

First, about the weather. "This is the land of extremes," says Alan Branhagen of Powell Gardens. That's a surprise to people who move here.

They discover that one winter is mild and the next winter they may as well be living in Minnesota. That's hard on perennials, which may come back some years and may not others.

Next comes spring, always beautiful. It inspires people to go to the nursery and buy pansies and flowering cabbage, thinking they'll bloom all summer. After all, they're annuals. And indeed, they do just fine — until May.

That's when summer hits, and that's one season that's never a mystery. It's always hot. A new heat map puts Kansas City in the same zone as Atlanta, Branhagen says. "People tend to think we're more like Chicago or New York, but we're not," he says.

As a result, says Duane Hoover of Kauffman Memorial Garden, perennials may survive cold winters only to get burned out by hot summers. So don't take it personally.

"Our weather causes many things to fail that would generally be fine," Hoover says. "Failures are part of the adventure of gardening here."

The soil isn't much better. Most of us have to work with heavy, poorly drained clay.

Alan Branhagen of Powell Gardens in the prairie planting on the Island Garden.

"People who are new here say, 'We thought we'd moved into the middle of the Heartland where the best soil in the country is,'" Branhagen says. "Actually, it's cruddy."

But you can do more about the soil than the weather. If you dig in anything organic, such as peat moss, mulch or compost, it will help. You can even dig in rock and gravel to loosen the soil, but it won't provide any nutrients.

Avoid the temptation of simply adding some sand, Branhagen says, because clay and sand mix into concrete. At Powell, gardeners start a new bed by digging it up and filling it back in with 3/4 original soil and 1/4 compost. Sometimes they add pine bark.

Duane Hoover of Kauffman Memorial Garden, with `Blue Bog' salvia in the foreground.

Annuals

If you're looking for success, don't ignore the commonplace plants. Tried-and-true annuals generally work well in Kansas City, including marigolds, salvia, petunias and geraniums, Hoover says.

And they'll look good through the summer if you give them enough water in the early heat in June. Don't wait until the panic of the first 95-degree day to get serious about watering. You need to keep your flowers in good health before the stress hits. That's "PHC," or plant health care, which Hoover says is a concept being used more now in gardening. Most annuals also need a lot of fertilizing, too — at least every other week in the summer.

If you're looking for something a little different that will survive August, Hoover recommends angelonia, a newer annual that's not used a lot yet. It thrives in partial sun, with early morning and late evening sun being ideal. The angelonias at Kauffman Garden are in a bed, but most home gardeners use them in pots.

Below, New England aster. Right, rough Blazing Star.

Perennials

Gardeners, even new ones, can't go wrong by trying the perennial plants of the year, Branhagen says. Those flowers have been tested and have proved themselves to be long-blooming and tough. You can find a list of plants of the year at better garden centers or on the Internet. The Perennial Plant Association maintains the list at www.perennialplant.org.

But Branhagen also says he likes to promote native and more regional plants for Kansas City gardeners. "Why go to New York and see the same things over and over?" he asks. "I like to celebrate what we have."

Among the many resources for native plants is a web site, www.grownative.org, which suggests Missouri natives and even helps you find them. The book *The Landscaping Revolution* by Andy Wasowski is also a good read, Branhagen says.

Spring Favorites

Among our experts' favorite spring-blooming perennials for Kansas City are Virginia bluebells and wild phlox, or sweet william. Two others:

Baptisia, also called blue false indigo. It has a blue, spiky bloom in early to mid-spring, leaving a 2-foot-tall plant that is vigorous and will take the heat. Baptisia has interesting seed pods in the fall, but when the plant starts to look ratty and brown, Hoover cuts it back.

Old-fashioned peonies. They're tried and true, and when they're done blooming you still have good foliage through the summer. Hoover prefers single-flowered varieties a little more than doubles, if only because they don't get as heavy in the rain and flop as much. Singles are actually older varieties than doubles, he says.

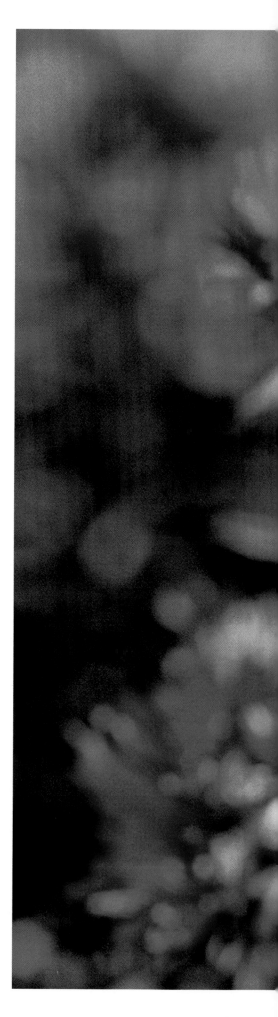

'Alma Porschke' aster which actually blooms in the fall.

'Goldsturm' rudbeckia.

Summer Favorites

Among the experts' favorite summer-blooming perennials for Kansas City:

Purple coneflowers. Almost any variety is tough enough to do well in this area, Branhagen says, but the pale purple coneflower is a native and is underutilized. The pale purple actually prefers the rainfall we get, so it requires no extra water or fertilizer. The yellow purple coneflower is another interesting variety that grows wild in the Ozarks and prefers our natural conditions. But gardeners use it more in the East than here. "It makes me crazy," Branhagen says. Other varieties are great too, though, including a Tennessee hybrid that is excellent in heat and drought. Some more common varieties actually like some shade and more moist conditions, Branhagen has found. He recommends leaving the seed heads on for butterflies and for bird food, especially for finches. And if the heads stay on over the winter they create an interesting effect by catching the snow.

Rudbeckia (black-eyed susans). They are tremendous for this area, they bloom a long time and there are many species. Their only problem is that they can seed so much, so you need to be sure they don't overrun your garden. One of the most popular varieties is Goldsturm.

Walker's low catmint. It's so tough you can't damage it, Branhagen says. It has gray flowers on blue-gray foliage, and

Moonbeam coreopsis. It works incredibly well in this area, blooming vigorously through much of the summer, Hoover says. Other than requiring full sun, it's carefree. You can divide it in the spring every two or three years if you want, but you don't need to.

Asters. These are actually fall bloomers, but Branhagen says they're easy and underused. The aromatic and New England asters are especially good here, he says. The New England asters need to be cut back by half in mid-summer to keep them from growing 8 feet tall. Purple Dome is a good, more compact variety that doesn't have a tendency to flop.

Autumn joy sedum. Another great fall bloomer. If it gets floppy, you might be giving it too much water and fertilizer. If so, cut it back in mid-summer. Although it's often listed as full sun, it can take more shade than you'd think, Branhagen says. The seed heads also look good if you leave them on over the winter.

if you deadhead spent flowers it will rebloom, sometimes into October.

Blazing Stars (liatris). This is a native wildflower that's great for butterflies. The flowers are wands of purple that are unusual because they bloom from the top down. It has lots of varieties so you can sequence them to bloom from summer through fall. The cultivar, Kobold, is the first variety to bloom. The only problem is that they grow from corms, which voles, mice and chipmunks like to eat. If you have rodent problems, you can buy blazing stars already growing as plants. Or, since a bag of corms is relatively inexpensive, you can just plant a lot of them.

Garden phlox. These are old-fashioned plants that come in many varieties, including some new ones such as Shortwood (pink) and David (white). Shortwood can bloom through August. The newer varieties don't have nectar for butterflies, though. Heirloom varieties, which are native to the Ozarks, have nectar but don't bloom as long.

Walker's low catmint.

Trends

Several home gardening trends have taken off in recent years in this area.

Butterfly gardening. "That's exploded in the last five years," Branhagen says. See Page 112 for an example of a Kansas City butterfly garden.

Rock gardening. "It was popular in the 1920s and now it's becoming really popular again," Branhagen says. Most of the plants don't like extra water, and some are from the American Southwest, which is a popular look now.

Low-water gardening. Branhagen thinks that may be the hottest trend now — plants that can tolerate drought. The old term for it was xeriscaping, but that's not used as much anymore. Powell's island garden, now three years old, has lots of low-water plants.

Water gardening. The Kansas City-area water garden society is one of the biggest in the country, Branhagen says. And it makes sense. Water gardens lend themselves to our hot summers, plus a lot of the plants are relatively easy to grow. See Page 164 for a Kansas City water garden.

Meet the Experts

Alan Branhagen, director of horticulture at Powell Gardens, has gardened for 27 years — ever since he was 14. He has a bachelor's degree in landscape architecture from Iowa State University and a master's degree from Louisiana State. He has been at Powell Gardens for seven years.

Duane Hoover, horticulturist at Kauffman Memorial Garden, has a bachelor's degree in ornamental horticulture and plant pathology from Kansas State University. He was with Soil Service Garden Center for 16 years before joining Kauffman Garden in 1999, a year before it opened.

Index

**Boldfaced page numbers
indicate photos.**